MARKI
through effective
COMMUNICATION

by

Don Booth B.Sc, M.Sc

TUDOR
PUBLISHING

GW00854249

Dedication

This book is dedicated to the women in my life, namely my wife and three daughters, none of whom have shown a great interest in the subject of marketing. Despite this fact, two of them have jobs that require some marketing skills and they are in fact quite good at marketing in practice. Hopefully, after reading this text, they will be even better.

Acknowledgements

I would like to acknowledge the assistance given to me by Mrs Cicely Johnson for typing the first draft of my manuscript and Sheila Zimmer and her team for helping to make this book possible by turning my early draft into manageable text. I would also like to thank Daniel Fuller for his editorial assistance and Dr D W Brough for his support and encouragement.

© D. Booth 1992

First published in Great Britain by Tudor Business Publishing Limited. Sole distributors worldwide, Hodder and Stoughton (Publishers) Ltd, Mill Road, Dunton Green, Sevenoaks, Kent, TN13 2XX

British Library Cataloguing in Publication Data

Booth, Don
   Marketing through effective communication.
   1.Marketing. Communication
   I. Title   II. Series
   658.8

   ISBN 1–872807–30–5

All rights reserved. No part of this publication may be reproduced, stored in a retrieval system, or transmitted in any form or by any means, electronic, mechanical, photocopying, recording, or otherwise without prior permission of Tudor Business Publishing Ltd. at Stanton House, Eastham Village Road, Eastham, Wirral, Merseyside L62 8AD

Typeset by Deltatype Ltd, Ellesmere Port, Cheshire
Printed and bound by Billing & Sons Ltd, Worcester.

CONTENTS

INTRODUCTION

The intention of this book is to provide a complete guide to the methods available by which an organisation, be it small business, large company or public sector organisation, can communicate effectively with its potential customers or clients. The book has been designed with those employees involved in the marketing of such organisations in mind, although it will be of use to employees at all levels within the organisation, or those running their own business.

Effective communications and marketing should be at the forefront of any organisation because an organisation that is unable to market itself or communicate with its prospective clients will find itself lacking whilst its competitors are forging ahead in their respective markets. It is for this reason that selling organisations should learn how to utilise all of the communication methods appropriate to their needs and this, when combined with a high level of customer service, will help to ensure that the organisations continues to thrive.

Effective communication, in all its forms, within the market-place, is the key to increased profitability.

D. Booth 1992.

CHAPTER 1

COMMUNICATION AND MARKETING

Introduction:—

In order for a company to survive, it must sell its products and in order to sell its products, these products must be marketed effectively. A company can use many media in order to get its product noticed by the buying public. Examples of these media would be:—

- Advertising (T.V., Radio, Billboards),
- Exhibition and,
- Door to door sales.

These media, and several others, are discussed further in later chapters.

The question now is how to define marketing. Although we all have some knowledge of what marketing is, even if this is simply watching adverts on television, it is difficult to define marketing in a business perspective. A suitable definition is offered by Booth in his text "Principles of Strategic Marketing"(7). He describes marketing as:—

- A total business philosophy aimed at improving profit performance by identifying customer needs.
- Designing a current service or product to satisfy those needs, delivering it on time and providing a sound after-service.

Communication with the Customer

Business success depends upon several factors, not least of which is having a good product to market in the first place. There are, however, many other factors that help an organisation become successful: determination to succeed, a steady input of money, possibly a little luck and basic communication skills. in order to maximise its profits, the organisation must communicate its image to prospective buyers in the most effective way it can, and this chapter deals with some of the fundamental considerations when communicating with prospects and potential buyers and outlines some of the more simple communication models.

Marketing was described by Bartles (1) as "A twofold process involving both technical and social factors". This is illustrated in the marketing of innovative products which aims to alter the behaviour of the purchaser but, before this can be done, the potential buyer must pass through various stages of awareness before eventually buying the product.

The Stages of Buyer Awareness

It is critical that the marketer understands the various stages of buyer readiness and is able to determine the stage at which a potential buyer is at any one time. The three basic stages are the cognitive stage, the effective stage and the action stage. at the cognitive stage, the buyer becomes aware of the product and has his or her attention drawn to it. Following this comes the effective stage, at which, the buyer has all of their attention focussed upon the product being marketed and begins to like what they are seeing. Finally comes the action stage at which the buyer makes the decision whether to buy or not to buy.

An important concept to understand at this point is that of the Decision Making Unit (D.M.U.), which, for most household products, will be the consumer. However, when discussing industrial buyer behaviour, it is necessary to understand that the Decision Making Unit may not be just one person, but

rather, it will be made up of several members of the organisation. These may include:—

- The User;
- The Specifier;
- The Sanctioners ie. Accountant, Purchasing Officers;
- The Chief Executive.

Webster and Wind in their text "A General Model for
nderstanding Buyer Behaviour" comment that "buying
usually involves many people in the decision making process as
well as individual and organisational goals".

Communication Models:—

The diagram below (Diagram 1) draws attention to several
"models" that may help in understanding the communication
process. The table shows three different models and, although
they do differ in certain aspects, they all show that every buyer
passes through the three stages illustrated earlier, and the
events that occur within the buyer's subconscious in each of
these stages.

Diagram 1

RESPONSE HIERARCHY MODELS

STAGES	AIDA (3) model	Hierarchy – (4) of – effects model	Innovation – Adoption model
COGNITIVE	Attention ↓	Awareness ↓ Knowledge ↓	Awareness ↓
AFFECTIVE	Interest ↓ Desire	Liking ↓ Preference ↓ Conviction	Interest ↓ Evaluation
CONATIVE	Action	Purchase	Trial ↓ Adoption

In the AIDA (Attention, Interest, Desire, Action) model, the buyer's attention is drawn to the product in the cognitive stage. As the buyer enters the effective stage, his or her interest in the product increases until they begin to desire it. Finally, the buyer enters the action stage at which a purchase will take place.

With the "Hierarchy of Effects" model, each event builds up through the buyer awareness stages — awareness becomes knowledge and knowledge becomes liking and so on until a purchase is made.

The "Innovation Adoption" model applies mainly, as its title would suggest to new products. The buyer will become aware of the product and this will lead to an interest in it. After the interest comes the evaluation stage at which the buyer will attempt to decide whether the product suits his or her needs. If the buyer decides that the product is what he or she is looking for, they may well take it for a trial period, in order to see if their evaluation was correct and, should this be the case, their company may adopt the product.

Interpersonal Communication:—

The basic aim of the communication process within the market place and within marketing itself is to provide answers to the questions

- Who is to say what?
- In which communication channel?
- To whom and with what effect?

These fundamental questions may be rephrased as a description of communications as consisting of a sender transmitting a message via media to a receiver who responds. however, such models are not intended to convey the idea of a purely passive audience because, in fact, the receiving audience may initiate or control the feedback to the sender, thus taking on the role of sender and playing an active part in communication, along with the marketer.

When attempting to market a product, the communicator

should focus attention on the elements that require a decision for example:—

- Who is the target audience?
- What response is sought?
- What message is to be developed?
- What feedback should be collected?

Before making a buying decision, the purchaser needs three types of information and so, when attempting to sell a product, the seller should focus upon supplying the buyer with this information. These forms of information are:—

- Information about the products existence and availability;
- Information that provides the buyer with a REASON for becoming interested in the product and;
- Information which assists in evaluating the product in terms of satisfying the needs of the potential purchaser.

There are three "channels" of information available to the potential buyer that will, in combination, satisfy his or her need for information. These are:—

- Marketer dominated channels — Those means of communication that are under the direct control of the marketer, such as the product itself, advertising, promotion, distribution and personal selling;
- Consumer dominated channels — Those interpersonal sources that are not under the direct control of the marketer, such as, recommendations by another;
- Neutral channels — Those channels that are not directly influenced by either the marketer or the consumer. Examples of neutral channels would be consumer reports, newspaper articles and information from various government agencies.

Information Flow:—

A good deal of research and literature, mainly in the

academic journals, deals with the two-step flow of information which provides the link between the mass media and interpersonal communications. This concept, modified over the years, suggests that information and ideas flow from "change agents" to the less active sections of the population. This two-step flow adds an intermediary point, the "opinion leader", to the communication process. Therefore, it is suggested that information is fed by change agents to opinion leaders who, in turn, influence the more passive audience segment. This process is illustrated in Diagram 2 below:—

Diagram 2

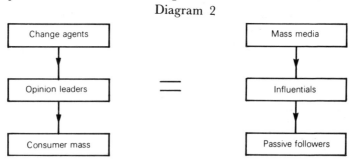

This simple two-step flow suggests that people receive information from interpersonal sources, instead of, or in addition to, mass media sources. The initiative in the transmission of information is assumed to lie with the communicator.

It is generally believed that, of the two information sources (formal and interpersonal) within the consumer dominated channel, the interpersonal source has the greatest influence on buyer behaviour and so the marketer must bear this in mind when considering the problem of stimulating opinion leaders. This matter will be dealt with in greater detail a little later on. Because of this, the two-step concept provides only a partial picture of the way in which the audience obtains information — friends and other interpersonal sources are generally deemed to be the more trustworthy, even if not particularly knowledgeable whereas neutral sources are deemed to be both more trustworthy and more knowledgeable. It may be concluded therefore, that, in providing information to create awareness and knowledge, the marketer dominated channels must play a major role, particularly since audiences are often seekers of specialist information about a product, especially where:—

- The product investment is high;
- The perceived risk is high and;
- The product has significant social and symbolic value.

An example of this intense information seeking would be a farmer considering the purchase of a piece of innovative and expensive machinery.

In the light of this information, the simple, two step model may be redrawn thus:—

Diagram 3

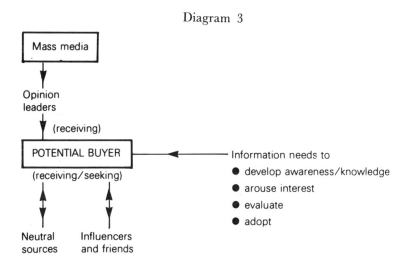

Small and Large Organisations

At this point it is worthwhile noting some of the ways in which communication characteristics differ between the small and

large company in order that the reader can have some help in
defending those characteristics best suited to their situation:—

SMALL COMPANY	LARGE COMPANY
• Loose task structure	• Job description for everyone
• Communication is informal	• Communication is formalised
• Limited knowledge of business environment	• Wide knowledge of business environment
• Wide range of management skills required in one person	• High specialist skill required
• Motivation of company is highly personalised and subject to personal preference	• Motivation of individual from broader base than company performance

Two further characteristics that may be exhibited by small
organisations are:—

- The smaller company offering jobs built around a person,
  rather than there being a formal job description as with
  larger companies and;
- Hostile or submissive attitudes towards their environment for example, a hostile attitude towards Governments, Colleges, Polytechnics and Universities.

The Importance of Integrating Methods:—

The integrated approach towards communicating with potential buyers should be stressed as an important marketing tool.
Many firms arrive at a total communications budget by little
more than guess work. Sometimes a sum of money based upon
last years sales income is used or, alternatively, what the
Finance Director deems affordable. Some firms use a figure
based upon an estimated competition budget or on the
"collective wisdom" of the industry. Larger firms that have a
sophisticated marketing function regard such guess work as

nonsense and direct their communication efforts by setting targets so that, if these targets are not reached, corrective action can be taken. This topic is discussed in greater detail under "Personal Selling and Advertising" later in this book.

SUMMARY

- Business success depends upon having the ability to employ basic communication and marketing skills effectively;
- There are three stages of buyer awareness — the cognitive, effective and action stages;
- The Decision Making Unit (D.M.U) can be just one person or a collection of people;
- Interpersonal Communication consists of a sender transmitting a message via media to a receiver who responds;
- There are three channels of information at the buyers disposal — marketer dominated, consumer dominated and neutral;
- Information usually flows from change agents through opinion leaders to the consumer mass;
- The consumer dominated, interpersonal channel has the greatest influence over the buyer;
- The organisation must integrate all of these methods into their overall business plan.

REFERENCES AND FURTHER READING

Bartles, R. *Journal of Marketing* (Vol. 32) July 1968.

Lasswell, D.H. *Power and Personality*. Norton and Company, New York.

Kotler, P. *Marketing Management 4th Ed* Prentice Hall 1972.

Webster and Wind. *A General Model For Understanding Buyer Behaviour. Journal of Marketing* (Vol 34) April 1972.

Pettigrew, A. *The Industrial Purchasing Decision As A Potential Process* Journal of Marketing, Spring 1975.

Morrison, R. *A Comtemporary Ode: The Joy of Marketing* The Times Saturday Review. August 11, 1990.

CHAPTER 2

COMMUNICATION WITHIN THE MARKETING FUNCTION

Introduction

Effective communication within any department is a prerequisite for the effective functioning of that department. This is certainly true for the Marketing function. Unless it can communicate effectively with itself, how can it possibly communicate with other departments within its own organisation, and with other organisations? This chapter will examine how such internal communication may best be achieved through effective team meetings in general and the technique known as Team Briefing in particular.

Communication

The word "communication" derives from the Latin, as do the words "communion", "community", "communal", and many others. They are all about being as one or sharing, and sharing suggests a two-way process. For example we can talk to somebody and they can listen. However, if there is no feedback from the listener to talker, the talker may not know if he/she has effectively communicated with or simply transmitted to that listener. Thus effective communication needs to be a two-way process and may be defined as:

The exchanging and imparting of information in order to gain

understanding and perhaps promote action. Many organisations, and departments within organisations, find such two-
way communication can best be achieved through a technique
known as team briefing. The Industrial Society is recognised as
the leading light in such matters and further information on
Team Briefing may be obtained from them.(1)

Team Briefing

Team briefing is a systematic yet flexible drill for regularly
communicating to all employees decisions and plans which
affect them or information which may be of interest to them.(2)
There are no hard and fast rules for effective briefing which
must be slavishly followed. Rather there are several guiding
principles which, if followed as closely as the constraints
imposed by the organisation permit, should help the participating department or organisation to effect an improvement in
the way it communicates with its staff. These guiding principles
are as follows:

Face-to-Face

Albert Mehrabian(3) found that effective face-to-face communication was down to three functions, namely

- the words used by the speaker (known as 'verbal')
- the tone of voice adopted by the speaker (known as 'vocal')
- the visual appearance of the speaker (known as 'visual')

He found from research that their respective contributions to
the total message are as follows:

- verbal (in words)   7%
- vocal (in tone)   38%
- visual (in body language) 55%

                           100%

It has been suggested that former Prime Minister Margaret

Thatcher's image was enhanced by softening her tone of voice and by changing her physical appearance. The words she spoke, it may be argued, were largely left unchanged.

Obviously face-to-face communication means that all three elements can be utilised and used to good effect. Whilst, of course, there will always be a place for the written word and the telephone, one cannot ask questions of the former and one cannot read other's gestures when using the latter.

In short, face-to-face communication permits two-way-communication.

In Teams

A team may be defined as a group of people working towards a common objective or objectives. Communication face-to-face in teams means that all those present should receive the same message at the same time, thus helping to prevent misunderstanding. Using a sporting analogy, the football or hockey coach talks to the team as a team before the game, at half-time and after the game, about team issues. So too with the Marketing function. There is no way a group of people can be built into and maintained as a cohesive team without them being brought together to discuss common team issues. The size of the team is also an important consideration. For example it is more difficult to hold a meaningful team meeting with a team of, say 40 people, than it is with a team of only 12. It is recommended that the ideal team should comprise something between 4 and 15 members. Again the Sports analogy makes the point clearly; football teams vary in size between 11 and 15 players depending on the code of the game concerned.

By the Team Leader

The team leader – the person immediately accountable for the performance of the team – is the person who should be briefing the team, face-to-face. This is so for essentially two reasons:-

(a) The team leader's status as the leader of that team should be enhanced or reinforced by regularly communicating to that team about team issues. The old adage that he or she who communicates is he or she who leads is certainly borne out of reality. For example, many people still perceive Mr Derek Hatton to have been the leader of the Liverpool City Council during the mid-1980s when in fact he was deputy to Mr John Hamilton. The former was seen speaking more in public than the latter and so Mr Hatton was often perceived by the public to be the leader.

(b) The team leader is more likely to speak the language of the team than is, say, the team leader's boss's boss. Using the family analogy, father/mother is more likely to speak the language of the nuclear family than is, say, great-grandfather/mother.

Regular

Whilst the frequency for holding such team meetings varies from organisation to organisation, the important factor is that they are conducted on a regular basis. For example, many Japanese organisations (both here and in Japan) hold regular daily team meetings at the start of the working day. The Industrial Society advocates such meetings should be held at least monthly, for about 30 minutes, with a calendar of dates set out to ensure they take place. The danger of not holding such meetings regularly is that they might only be held in times of crisis. In an attempt to market a significantly different product from its usual range, an engineering company decided to discuss progress with its staff every fortnight. The information was so well received that after the successful launch of the product regular monthly meetings continued and became part of the more open culture of that company.

   In short, it is difficult to expect people to trust the information if they are only ever assembled together to hear bad news.

Relevant

It is extremely important to ensure that the information discussed at the team meeting is relevant to that particular team. Whilst there may be information that the Chief Executive wants everyone in the organisation to know about, there should also be information local to each team and generated by the leader of that team.

For example, the successful launch of an entirely new concept in marketing may well be of interest to the whole staff. However the response rate to a particular survey by, say field services department, may only be relevant to members of that department.

In short, the information must be relevant and of interest to those receiving that information, otherwise it will be a case of holding meetings for the sake of holding them.

Monitored

Like all management systems, Team Briefing should be monitored, to ensure it is happening and taking place effectively.

A senior manager may sit in on a briefing session conducted by one of his/her junior managers, to see how it is being conducted and received. Similarly, senior managers should walk the place of work regularly and talk to employees. In so doing they can check if the information is being received clearly by such staff via their monthly briefing sessions.

The Subjects for Team Briefing

So as to perform effectively as members of their teams, people need to know various things about their team in particular and the wider organisation in general. The subjects for effective briefings may be grouped for convenience under four broad headings, as follows:-

Progress and Performance

People need to know how they are doing at three levels.

- as individuals
- as a department/team
- as an organisation

The first should be the subject of appraisals and one-to-one sessions. The last two fit nicely into the scope of Team Briefing.

People can only give of their best if they know how they are doing. Returning to the sporting analogy, the team needs to know whether it has won or lost the match. So too at work. People in teams and organisations need to know if they have had a successful month or a less than successful month. For example, various marketing functions will need to know how they are doing in terms of completing a survey on time, whether or not they have mailed their target audience on time or whether the results of the market survey have been warmly received by the client. In addition to such local team issues people may benefit from knowing more global-type information about how the parent organisation is fairing in its "fight" with competitors for acquiring certain key accounts.

In short, people need to know the score at end of the match, together with their position in the league table.

Policy

Policy-type issues may also have to be communicated to staff. For example, new policies being adopted, new procedures to be followed, new corporate visions being formulated, new structures being developed all have be be explained clearly to the staff. It is not sufficient just to tell people what these are; it has to be clearly explained why and how they will be executed or achieved.

People

For most people in employment today, work is a social situation. People need to know about people. They need to know about visitors, about changes in personnel, about personal successes, about social issues.

Points for Action

If people need to know how they performed as a team last month (under Progress) it follows logically that they should have clear indications of what is required of them in the coming month. What their priorities are for next month. Anything that needs improving upon. Earlier in the chapter effective communication was defined as the exchanging and imparting of information to gain understanding and promote some sort of action. If action can be achieved via Points for Action then the whole process of Team Briefing becomes dynamic and results orientated. That should be for the benefit of any function/ department at work.

The Benefits

A basic tenet of marketing is that people act to benefit, not to lose. It follows, therefore, that it is important to highlight some of the benefits likely to result from an effective system of team briefings.

Same Message To All

Getting the team together to pass on information means they all receive the same message at the same time. They all benefit from the questions asked and subsequent answers given. This means that misunderstandings can be reduced, as the briefer is able to check the basic understanding of the message with each member present.

Disarms the Grapevine

The grapevine – passing on of information by people who cannot be held accountable for it – can be extremely destructive. Team Briefing requires the briefer to take accountability for the information and to either refute or confirm the validity of such rumours. This should go some way to minimising the destructive effects of current rumours.

Helps to increase commitment

Regular breifing affords the opportunity for the leader to remind the team just how important their contribution is to the well-being of the organisation. People are not born to know their contribution is vital; they have to be reminded regularly by their leader. In so doing their commitment to the department and the organisation may well be increased.

Helps increase co-operation with change

Many people dislike change and feel threatened by it. However if the need for the change is clearly explained, and if they are given regular updates on the progress of the changes, they are more likely to accept the change.

Reinforces Management role

To repeat, he/she who communicates is he/she who leads. Effective briefing by the leader of the team is as much to do with effective leadership as it is to do with effective communication.

Improves the quality of consultation

Briefing is essentially about keeping people better informed. When their views are sought through the consultation process they are more likely to have a positive contribution to make if they are aware of what's going on around them.

These then are some of the benefits likely to result from implementing an effective briefing system.

Tips for Positive Briefing

The briefing process can be divided into 3 stages:

- before the briefing
- during the briefing
- at the end

There now follows some tips on helping to make the briefing system a success.

Before the Briefing

(a) Collect information throughout the month.
(b) Prepare briefing notes using a headlines and notes format.
(c) Adopt a television news format for the briefing. i.e. Brief headlines, then content followed by a brief summary.
(d) Advise the team that they may ask questions relevant to the briefing.
(e) Ensure the briefing session will not be interrupted.

During the Briefing

(a) Use the language of the team.
(b) Show commitment to items which the briefer may privately disagree with.
(c) Relate as much as possible to the team's department.
(d) Keep to the time allocated.
(e) Be enthusiastic; it can be infectious.

At the End

(a) Invite final questions before summarising.
(b) Give a brief summary of main points.
(c) Advise when the next briefing session will take place.

SUMMARY

Team briefing will not solve all of the problems associated with communication but should go some way to effecting an improvement. Effective briefing should be seen as beneficial to all; the organisation itself, its management and staff and its customers and clients.

FURTHER INFORMATION

1. The Industrial Society, Peter Runge House, Carlton House Terrace, London SW1Y 5DG

REFERENCES

2. "Team Briefing" by Janis Grummitt (Industrial Society, 1983)
3. "Body language – how to read others' thoughts by their gestures" by Allan Pease (Sheldon Press, 1981)

CHAPTER 3

DIRECTORIES

Introduction:—

The following chapters outline some of the more common methods of communicating with the customer. Each method is dealt with in a separate chapter with a summary, further reading and reference addresses included at the end.

Directories provide a cost effective method for promoting both a firm's name and it's products. Readers are, generally, good prospects because they are usually looking for something specific and are therefore paying close attention to the text. This means that, if a firm has a highly visible entry, it will catch the readers eye and will stick in their minds so that, even if the reader is not looking for that particular service at the time, they will remember the entry and return to it when they are looking for that service. When potential customers refer to a directory, they usually have a problem and are looking for help in solving it, some directories will be essential for most people at one time or another, thus ensuring that an entry will be seen by a large number of potential buyers; especially since an entry can be seen 365 days of the year, even if the directory is several years old.

A firm appearing in the ordinary telephone directory must ensure that it's name appears without misprints or other errors, as this could well damage its image. If the firm's name has a difficult spelling, it may be worth while getting two entries, one in very bold type, in order to ensure that the name is not scanned over: since the first entry in the telephone book is free, the second entry will be relatively cheap. The cost, at the time of writing, of advertising in bold surround is £3 per quarter with an initial £15 "setting-up" charge. A "super bold" entry costs £10 per quarter, again with the initial £15 "setting-up" fee.

A large firm may have a catchment area that covers several regions so, in this situation, the firm would be well advised to place entries in the telephone books that cover all of those regions. Enquiries about telephone listings for the 103 U.K. directories are dealt with by the Directory Entry Section of the local British Telecom area office.

British Telecom, in it's free publication "Business Catalogue", gives information on the use of directories and details of the size and scope of "Yellow Pages" as well as it's other means of helping the business user through "Business Pages", "Yellow Pages Guides", "Electronic Yellow Pages" and "Talking Pages".

"Yellow Pages" is Britain's most comprehensive classified directory since every business in the country with a telephone number gets a free listing and is delivered to all houses and businesses with a telephone line. The listing of a business means easy, direct access to it's market — 40% of all adults and 95% of all business people will have used "Yellow Pages" within the past 4 weeks in order to find a particular product or service they required, in fact, "Yellow Pages" is classed by many as an invaluable source of information, There are 66 directories available nationwide and advertising costs can be obtained by contacting ITT WORLD DIRECTORIES (1).

"CRONERS A — Z OF BUSINESS INFORMATION SOURCES" is available in the reference section of most libraries and provides information from trade directories, thus saving time in retrieving publications and papers written by others. Croner's directory helps in summarising information often required by an enterprise, and, details essential basic business information. The directory has been compiled with the non-information specialist in mind and, for this reason, it has been set out in alphabetical order by subject area and then alphabetically by source. For each entry there is a telephone number which will allow the user to further pursue sources that interest them. Copies of the directory and further details can be obtained from — croner publications limited)2).

JORDANS REGIONAL DIRECTORIES provide information on at least 1000 companies registered in each region and, for many of these companies, three year financial profiles are provided. These profiles give a summary of profit and loss accounts, balance sheets, numbers of employees and profitability. So, should a reader wish to contact potential clients through telemarketing, or in person they can be adequately prepared. In addition, business descriptions are provided to enable marketers to identify companies in specific industries. Literature can be obtained by contacting Jordan and Sons Limited (3).

KELLY'S BUSINESS DIRECTORY is one of the U.K's leading industrial guides presented in one, easy to use, volume. This comprehensive, up to date, directory provides valuable business information including company addresses and tele-communication details. The directory is cross referenced alphabetically and by product or service. In the 1990 edition there are some 84,000 companies, covering the whole of the British industry. This directory can help when it comes to :—

- Locating new suppliers;
- Checking communication details;
- Compiling mail shots;
- Researching competitors and marketing trends and;
- Targeting new sales contacts.

Further details can be obtained from Kelly's Directories (4).
KOMPASS. Kompass directories are published in association with the Confederation of British Industry and contain comprehensive information on well over 37,000 different U.K. companies and more than 41,000 different products and

services together with financial information needed to make accurate business decisions. The directory comes in four volumes that can be purchased separately or together and is available from Kompass Publishers (5)

THOMPSON LOCAL DIRECTORIES are particularly useful for reaching local customers — 143 local directories cover 30 million consumers nationwide. Directories are delivered, free of charge, to 95% of homes and businesses in each of the directory areas. The directory numbers, circulation statistics, rate bands and advertising costs are available from Thompson Directories (6).

REFERENCE ADDRESSES

1. ITT World Directories
   Jackson House
   4th Floor
   Gibson Road
   Sale
   Cheshire   Tel. 061–969 3666

2. Croner Publications Limited
   M/90 Croner House
   London Road
   Kingston-Upon-Thames
   Surrey
   KT2 6SR

3. Jordan and Sons Limited
   21, St Thomas Street
   Bristol
   BS1 6JS   Tel. 0272—230600

4. Kelly's Directories
   The Marketing and Sales Manager
   Windsor Court
   East Grinstead House
   East Grinstead
   West Sussex
   RH19 1XA   Tel. 0342—326972, FAX. 0342—315130

5. Kompass Publishers
   Windsor Court
   East Grimstead House
   East Grimstead
   West Sussex
   RH19 1XD

6. Thompson Directories
   296 Farnborough Road
   Farnborough
   Hants
   GU14 7NU   Tel. 0252—561111

CHAPTER 4

DIRECT MAIL

Introduction

Door to door distribution of mailshots is becoming increasingly common and provides an important advertising medium for many firms. It is an independent, low cost method of targeting a selected customer base. This method can be used to:—

- Advertise specific products;
- Produce sales leads;
- Provide Market Research information;
- Maintain customer contact and;
- Test new products or packaging types.

The use of a reply device can help a firm gain valuable information concerning customer needs and provides a rapid measure of the effectiveness of an advertising campaign.

A large firm may well use the Post Office as a means of delivering literature to either households or businesses and the initial outlay of £43 per thousand items mailed is soon recouped through the increased sales. More information on this service can be obtained through the Local Postal Service representative or the Area Business Customer Care Unit of the Post Office.

Rather than use the advice of large organisations such as the Post Office, small firms are advised to attempt their own mailshot, since this will help them to focus some attention on initial matters such as:—

- Precisely who to address within their selected market segment (s);
- How their product or service fulfils the needs of the prospects and;
- How the response rate for mailings can be improved.

Direct Mail is the U.K.'s third largest advertising medium in terms of annual expenditure (as Diagram 2 shows) and has increased rapidly in actual volume over the past years (Diagram 1). Factors accounting for this rapid increase in the use, and acceptance of, direct mail are:—

- Fragmentation of the media. There are now two commercial channels, cable television and satellite television, which makes it much harder for large organisations to advertise adequately on television, and;
- An increase in "free-sheets" alongside thetraditional "paid for" local press.

Under these circumstances, Direct Mail's ability to not only locate and reach a target market, but to discriminate between various sections of the market, begin to look increasingly attractive.

Source: Advertising Association Statistics		Diagram 1	
	1975	1985	GROWTH RATE
Consumer	280	925	+ 230%
Business to Business	260	378	+ 45%
TOTAL	540	1303	+ 141%

DIRECT MAIL VOLUME GROWTH
(FIGURES IN MILLIONS OF ITEMS MAILED)

Types of Direct Mailing:—

There are two types of direct mailing:—

- Consumer Direct Mail, and
- Business Direct Mail.

These will each be dealt with separately.

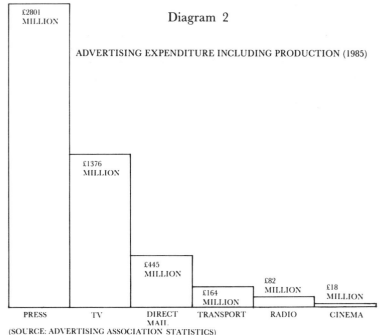

Diagram 2

ADVERTISING EXPENDITURE INCLUDING PRODUCTION (1985)

(SOURCE: ADVERTISING ASSOCIATION STATISTICS)

Consumer Direct Mail:—

The reasons for using consumer direct mail are varied. However, a list of the more common uses is as follows:—

Selling Direct:

Direct Mail is a medium for selling products direct to customers without the need for "middle men". The organisation can describe the product (or service) fully, and provide order facilities which come straight back to the firm.

Sales Lead Generation:

If the product requires a meeting between customers and one of the firm's salesforce (for example, fitted kitchens, central heating, insurance, etc), then Direct Mail makes it easy to get good, qualified leads for sales people.

Sales Promotion:

Direct Mail can get promotional messages, "money off" vouchers, special offers etc., to the correct recipients. Sales promotion by direct mail offers a way of getting customers to visit a store or showroom whilst still retaining a measure of control over the exposure of the promotion.

Clubs:

Book Clubs are perhaps the best known example of the use of Direct Mail as a convenient medium of communication and transaction between a club and its members. However, products other than books may be marketed by the club system. It is likely that these products will be "collectables" of some type — for example, records, porcelain miniatures, commemorative medallions etc.

Mail Order:

Many mail order traders use Direct Mail to successfully recruit new customers and local agents. It can also be used to sell direct.

Fund raising:

Direct Mail's ability to communicate personally with an individual makes it a powerful method of raising money for, say, a charitable organisation. It can carry the long copy often needed to convince the recipient of the worthiness of the charity and make it easy for the reader to respond with a donation.

Dealer Mailings:

If a firm's product is sold through dealers of any sort, then Direct Mail could be the right medium for them to use in order to reach the prospective customers in their particular catchment area.

"Follow-up" Mailings:

Keeping the company's name lodged firmly in the customers mind can be achieved by following up any kind of sales activity with a mailing. For example, checking that the customer is satisfied with his or her purchase, pointing out that something they bought last year is coming up for its annual service, or that they now have enough in their savings account to buy something. Using Direct Mail in this way can substantially increase sales by getting customers to think of the particular marketing company rather than other firms.

Business Direct Mail:

Business markets are typically made up of quite tightly defined, discrete groups of people who may not best be reached by mass advertising media. Direct Mail's ability to "zero-in" accurately on differing market sectors, and provide a message appropriate to each sector, makes it suitable for most business marketing and advertising tasks. Some of the more common of these are:-

Product Launch:

Often the launch of a new industrial product or business service entails getting the seller's message to the small, but very significant, number of people who will influence buying decisions or revise their own specifications (for example, specifying architects, senior company engineers, fleet managers, catering managers). Direct Mail can identify these people accurately, and help the marketer to get the full story across.

Sales Lead Generation:

Because industrial and business salespeople tend to be expensive to keep on the road, it is important to maximise their sales opportunities and time management whilst minimising wasted calls. Direct Mail can get warm sales leads for the salesforce, as well as doing some initial selling for them.

Dealer Support:

Direct Mail makes it easy to keep dealers, retail outlets, franchise holders fully informed about such things as marketing plans and to invite them to take part in, for example, any incentive schemes which may be in operation.

Conferences:

Business and trade conferences are now well established as a means of communicating with the firm's market or holding discussions with colleagues in the industry. Direct Mail is an ideal medium for inviting potential delegates particularly if the seller is looking for specific types of people in specific business sections.

Using the Firm's Customer Base:

Because so much business takes the form of repeat sales to existing customers and because the firm knows who these people are from client and sales records, contracts, leasing or rental deals, it can be well worth while mailing them regularly in order to maintain their custom.

Mailing Lists:—

Before embarking upon a mailing, a company must have a mailing list — a list of names and addresses of customers that will receive a mail-shot. Mailing lists can be obtained from various sources or a firm can compile its own from existing customer records.

If your firm is offering a product, or service, that will be of use to the general public then the Electorial Register, available from the local Town Hall, is a valuable source of names and addresses. Using this, you will be able to reach everyone (providing that they are on the list) within the district.

Alternatively your firm may wish to hire a mailing list. There are many professional list compilers, most of whom can be contacted through local telephone directories, though these are of greater value to firms competing in a specialist market rather than in the general market.

The Envelope:—

The envelope is the first thing that the prospect will see as he or she receives your mailshot so it is vitally important that this is eyecatching, otherwise, the prospect will throw it in the bin without opening it. An example of an effective envelope is shown below:—

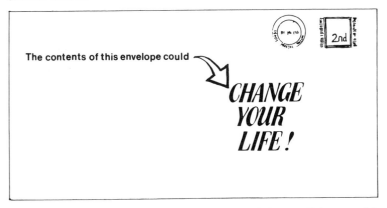

There is no way in which the recipient of the mailshot could miss the message given on the envelope and the promise that the contents could change the life of the recipient entices them to open the letter and read on....

Large organisations may use multicoloured envelopes with photographs or drawings on the front that are usually designed by an art department within the company but, if you are unable to afford this, the use of very large, bold letters with possibly one or two colours will prove just as effective for your organisation.

The Mailshot

There are several do's and dont's to consider when designing a mailshot. These are listed below:—

DO's —

- Always include illustrations even if it is only the company logo;
- Always address the prospect as if you are the solution to a problem they have;
- Always direct attention to the advantages of your product or services, for instance, environmentally friendly, cheaper than other methods etc;

- Always try to include a free offer or other incentive for the recipient, when he or she uses your services and;
- Always include a reply slip and freepost envelope — this will help you to gather information about the prospective clients.

DONT'S—

- Never use a mailshot that is too technical or verbose; it will bore the recipient and make them less willing to respond;
- Never humiliate the recipient or make them feel less intelligent then yourself, it gets their backs up;
- Never lie. If you lie about your product or service and are taken to court, your organisation will be in big trouble;
- Never deride the opposition;
- Never ask a prospect to write back to you. He or she cannot be bothered to write letters to you, nor pay for the stamp;
- Never insinuate that damage may occur through the prospect using your product or service and;
- Never leave large spaces on mailshots.

The two mailshots for an imaginary carpet cleaning firm that follow show how it should be done (Figure 1) and how not to do it (Figure 2). Judge for yourself which is the better!

The Reply Device:—

The inclusion of a means of reply to your mailshot is valuable since it will allow your company to judge how effective its mailing has been and gather information on which segments of the public are most interested in your product or services e.g. Housewifes, Businesspersons, the young or the elderly.

When designing the reply slip, be sure not to ask questions that are too personal as this may annoy the prospect and make them unwilling to fill in your form. The most personal a reply device should become is enquiring into such things as "Marital Status" or "Occupation", it should never ask about matters

Dear Householder,

How often have you looked at your carpet and wished that you could have it cleaned professionally without mess or fuss and without damage to your pocket?

PUNTERS CARPET CLEANERS offers a cheap, efficient carpet cleaning service that will leave your carpets looking as good as new.

Using the amazing new HOT WATER INJECTION SYSTEM we can clean your carpet thoroughly, removing ground in dirt, without any danger of your carpet shrinking and without the use of chemicals, so we are also ENVIRONMENT FRIENDLY.

"How much will this cost me?" we hear you cry. We will undercut the cheapest estimate you can find by 20% AND we offer you the chance to have an extra carpet cleaned for FREE, or, should you want all of your carpets cleaning we will reduce the price by the cost of cleaning your largest room.

For some more information, simply complete the short response slip included within this letter and return it, FREEPOST in the ready addressed envelope you will find enclosed.

Yours, Hoping to hear from you;

R.J. Punter

MANAGING DIRECTOR

Figure 1

Figure 2

Managing Director,
Punters Carpet Cleaners,
12, Acacia Avenue,
Hometon.

Dear Sir/Madam,

  Our company offers a superior carpet cleaning service with
which you will be most satisfied.

  Unlike other, poorer quality, carpet cleaning organisations
we offer the new Hot Water Injection system which can remove
all the dirt from carpets with a pile of 5 millimetres or less.
This new system works by forcing a mixture of hot water and
detergent directly into each carpet knot through a series of
tiny hollow needles that have a bore diameter of 0.005
millimetres. The carpet is then dried by the injection of hot
air into each knot through the same method.

  For more information write to the above address. The company
will not be held responsible for any damage that may be caused
to property during the process.

Yours Faithfully

R.J. Punter

MANAGING DIRECTOR

such as race or income. It is best not to offer an incentive to
return the reply slip since this will invalidate your research —
people will respond just to get the incentive rather than out of
genuine interest. A sample reply slip for "Punters Carpet
Cleaners" is shown below:—
Figure 3

PUNTERS CARPET CLEANERS

SEX .... M / F

AGE .... [ ]

Do you ..... Own your house [ ]
         Rent your house [ ]

No. of rooms 2 [ ]; 4 [ ]; 5 [ ]; 6 [ ]; more [ ]

Type of house DETACHED [ ]; SEMI [ ]; TERRACE [ ]

OCCUPATION --------------------------------
NAME ----------------------------------
ADDRESS --------------------------------

FURTHER DETAILS -------------------------- YES/NO

THANK YOU FOR YOUR HELP

The MULTIPLE RESPONSE type of reply is best since this
saves time for the prospect when filling in the slip and also saves
your organisation time since the information can be collated
easily. Remember to always be courteous — thank the recipient
for his or her help.

As a final point, always remember to leave enough space for
the recipient to reply. In Figure 3, you can see that only one
line has been left for the address. It is unlikely that an address
could be written on just one line and so this is likely to annoy the
prospect and make him or her less willing to fill in your form.

Testing:—

Now that you have your mailing list, eye-catching envelopes, user-friendly mailshot and a simple, effective response slip, you are ready to send out a TEST MAILING. This involves sending out a representative sample of mailshots and analysing the result before beginning a full scale mailing. In order to run a test and obtain valid results, it is necessary to mail to at least 5000 addresses on the list, otherwise the test is not worth running. This could mean that most of the addresses on your list, if your firm is small, have been mailed to. Should this be the case, you would be better advised to mail all of the addresses on your list and forget the test mailing.

Test mailing can be used to determine some of the following:—

- If the lists have too many errors and produce many "returned undelivered" mailings;
- If a rented list gets a better, worse or similar response as an in-house list;
- If the product pricing is sound. Is the price too high or too low?;
- If the inclusion of an offer or incentive makes a difference to the number of responses and;
- What portion of responses are converted to sales. Is this enough to meet profit targets?

The analysis of both the test and full mailings must be carried out thoroughly and accurately as the results can be used to improve subsequent mailings. The analysis can determine:—

- The best geographical locations for mailings;
- Which segments of the total market provide the best customers;
- The range of order values;
- The relationship between the cost of a sale and the profit made on that sale and;
- What cash flow patterns are to be expected in terms of payment.

If direct mailing is used properly it can be an effective means of both advertising a product and gaining some information about your customers.

SUMMARY

- Direct mail is an increasingly popular form of marketing
- There are two forms of direct mailing — consumer and business
- The envelope used should be eyecatching and pertinent to your product
- The mailshot should be friendly, it should stress the benefits, it should contain incentives and a reply device
- The mailshot should not belittle the recipient, be tooverbose or technical, contain lies or deride the opposition
- The reply device should be short, not too personal and easy to respond to.
- A test mailing of 5000 addresses can be used for larger lists. This can be a useful information gathering facility.

REFERENCES AND FURTHER READING

Royal Mail. *Guide to Effective Direct Mail* see Reference Addresses (1).

Royal Mail. *Direct Mail Information File* see Reference Addresses (2).

Jefkins, F. *The Secrets of Successful Direct Response Marketing.* Heinemann. 1988.

Booth, D. *Principles of Strategic Marketing.* Tudor Business Publishing Limited. September 1990

Fairlie, R. *Guide to Database Marketing and Direct Mail* Wyvern Business Library.

REFERENCE ADDRESSES

1. Post Office Direct Mail Department
   Post Office Headquarters
   33 Grosvenor Place
   SW1X 1PX

2. Head Office Post Office
   Royal Mail House
   Wellington Street
   Leeds
   LS1 1AA

3. The Direct Mail Producers Association
   34, Grant Avenue
   London
   N10 3BP   Tel 071–883 9854

4. The Direct Mail Services Standards Board
   23, Eccleston Street
   London
   SW1W 9PY   Tel 071–824 8651

5. The British Direct Marketing Association
   Grosvenor Gardens House
   Grosvenor Gardens
   London
   SW1W 0BJ   Tel 071–630 7322

APPENDIX 1

Measuring the Effectiveness of Direct Mail

1. The objective of any direct mail campaign must be clearly
   defined. It is the only basis on which any rational assessment of its success can be formed. With the objective clear,
   the next step must be to establish a budget — costs should be
   firmly controlled. The total cost must be set against the
   expected return from the mailing.
   (a) *One-off Costs*
   Writing and design work
   Finished artworks
   Photography
   Printing plate making
   These are fixed costs and are subject to firm quotations.
   These costs, can vary from £50 for a simple letter to over
   £1,000 for more complicated designs. An important point to
   make is that these costs should be funded from a central
   marketing budget and can thus be considered as part of total
   business overheads. Alternatively, the costs can be spread
   over the total projected mailing.
   (b) *On-Going Costs*
   Dependent upon the size and frequency of mailings:

	Cost Range Per 1000 (£'s)
Printing	30 — 200
Envelopes	5 — 15
The list	0 — 80
Enclosing and labelling	70 — 85
	110 — 395

Each of these can be costed seperately and it is possible to arrive at an overall budget, into which the component costs can be fitted. A fairly typical mailing cost is £200 per 1000 and this figure will be used in the calculation.

Generating Leads for Salesman

2. To calculate the *cost of Direct Mail per field sale*. The key considerations are:

    — *response rate* ie. number or recorded responses from the mailshot.

    — *conversion rate* ie the number of responses (measured as a percentage) that are converted to actual sales and the mailing cost per 1000

3. These factors are linked by the following formula:

    Cost of Direct Mail per sale =

    $$\frac{\text{Mailing cost per 1000}}{\text{Response rate \%}} \times \frac{10}{\text{Conversion rate \%}}$$

4. Taking an example:

    Mailing cost per 1000 = £200
    Response rate = 2%
    Conversion rate = 25%
    Then,

    $$\text{Cost of Direct Mail Per Sale} = \frac{200}{2} \times \frac{10}{25} = £40$$

This might seem expensive but compare the cost to the cost of a salesman's visit. Say the cost of a visit is £20. If his conversion rate is 1 in 4, then the cost of a successful sale would be £80!

5. *Learning Points*

    • Examine the cost of mailing. Why send out sales leaflets when a simple but effective letter will do the trick?

    • Increase response rate by offering a Business Reply or Freepost facility. Offer an incentive as well. Testing for a desired level of response is dealt with later.

    • Offer an incentive to boost the conversion rate: or send the salesman on a course.

Generating Sales for Mail Order

6. The secret here is to determine the profitability constraints and start by looking at how profit may be calculated.
7. Firstly, calculate gross contribution. This is the contribution the mailing makes on profit *before* the costs of the mailing have been taken into account. Simply:

Gross contribution = net order value — order cost

The net order value is the selling price less VAT but including postage and packing.

8. Assume that cash will be sent with the order, but nevertheless provision must be made for the following:
   — order processing
   — order picking and packing
   — refunds
   — returns including refurbishing and repacking
   — general ongoing administration
9. What next? Look at how the costs are related to response rate and gross contribution:

(Gross contribution × $\dfrac{\text{Response}}{\text{rate \%}}$ × 10)
(per order
__ Mailing cost = Profit/loss
(per 1000 per 1000

The next stage is to calculate what response rate is required to breakeven. Introducing some figures:

Net order value = £30 (eg an executive briefcase)
Order cost = £15 (imported from Taiwan)
Mailing cost = £200
Profit/Loss = 0 for breakeven
   Therefore:
   Gross contribution = 30 — 15 = 15
   Substituting in the formula gives:

(15 × Response rate % × 10) — 200 = 0
Therefore response rate % $\dfrac{200}{15 \times 10} = 1.33$

The table at Appendix A gives a simple way of calculating the response rate for breakeven for different values of gross contribution and mailing costs.

10. This means that so long as a response rate of 1.33% is achieved mailing costs will be covered. What about profitability? If a target of £5 per order is set the next stage is to calculate the response rate to achieve this:

(Gross contribution x Response rate % x 10) − Mailing cost per 100

= Response rate % of 10 x target profit per order

$(15 \times R10) - 200 = R \times 10 \times 5$

$150R - 200 = 50R$

$150R - 50R = 200$

$R = 2\%$

If a response rate of 2% is achieved, a profit of £5 per order will be made.

11. *Boosting Response*

It can be seen that profitability is dependent on the response rate. It follows that if an improved response rate can be achieved more profit can be made. If an additional leaflet is included (eg a testimonial) which costs £50 per 1000 but that this increases response rate by 3%. Let's look at the profit. Remember:

Profit per 1000 = Gross contribution x Response Rate % x 10 − Mailing cost per 1000

$= 15 \times 3 \times 10 - 250$

$= 450 - 250 = 200$

Number of responses per 1000 = 30

So,

Profitability = $\frac{200}{30}$ = £6.57 per order

12. *Learning Points*

• The higher the gross contribution or margin on the product, the lower the response rate required to breakeven

• Boosting response rate boosts profitability

• Use the formulae to calculate:

— response rate to breakeven
— response rate for a given level of profit
— effect of varying mailing costs and response rate
- Look for ways of increasing the margin eg. buying larger quantities, trimming admin costs
- Make sure the product is of good quality and matches the expectations of the customer. This will reduce returns
- Look for ways of reducing mailing costs:
— Larger mailings quality for poster for larger postage rebates (up to £30 per 1000)
— Printing costs also reduce with larger print runs
— Don't make unnecessary use of expensive printing two colours are often as good as four

13. *Testing for Success*

A maxim for direct mail is to test. Having done the sums on probability there is no point in mailing out to a list of 100,000 only to find that the response rate is 1% i.e. less than required for breakeven in the previous example. So how many should be mailed out in a test mail? Again mathematics provides the answer.

14. The size of the sample will depend upon:
- the expected response rate
- the % error, plus or minus, from the expected response rate, that you are prepared to tolerate
- — the confidence level required of the result. Most statisticians work to a confidence level of 95%

A formula for determining sample size is:

Sample size = Confidence level value × % response × % non—response
(% error)

For 95% confidence, the confidence level equals 3.85.

15. If the previous example is used and a 2% response is aimed for, the response should be no less than 1.5% to ensure that the response is not too near to breakeven. The error tolerance is therefore 0.5% and the target test response 2%. Sample size for a test shot can be calculated as follows:

Sample size = $\dfrac{3.84 \times 2 \times 98}{0.5 \times 0.5}$ = 3010.6

So test 3000

Let's be clear what this means. Using a test sample size of 3011, the response will fall between 1.5% and 2.5%, 95 times in every 100 mailed. So if response of only 1% is achieved, the main mailing would not go ahead thus avoiding an expensive failure. If 4% is achieved the firm may run out of stock.

16. To simplify the calculation, Table 2 enables the estimated test sample sizes for different response rates and error limits to be checked.

17. *Summary to Key Points*
    - Do the sums
    - Calculate the cost per sale or profit per response
    - Calculate a sample test size
    - Test the list

TABLE 1

Percentage response required to cover costs — breakeven — on a gross contribution of £1—£100 per order and a mailing cost of £100—£200 per 1000.

GROSS CON-TRIBUTION	MAILING COST £									
£	100	120	130	140	150	160	170	180	190	200
1	10.00	12.00	13.00	14.00	15.00	16.00	17.0C	18.00	19.00	20.00
2	5.00	6.00	6.50	7.00	7.50	8.00	8.50	9.00	9.50	10.00
3	3.33	4.00	4.33	4.67	5.00	5.33	5.67	6.00	6.33	6.67
4	2.50	3.00	3.25	3.50	3.75	4.00	4.25	4.50	4.75	5.00
5	2.00	2.40	2.60	2.80	3.00	3.20	3.40	3.60	3.80	4.00
6	1.67	2.00	2.17	2.33	2.50	2.67	2.83	3.00	3.17	3.33
7	1.43	1.71	1.86	2.00	2.14	2.29	2.43	2.57	2.71	2.86
8	1.25	1.50	1.63	1.75	1.88	2.00	2.13	2.25	2.38	2.50
9	1.11	1.33	1.44	1.56	1.67	1.78	1.89	2.00	2.11	2.22
10	1.00	1.20	1.30	1.40	1.50	1.60	1.70	1.80	1.90	2.00
11	0.91	1.09	1.18	1.27	1.36	1.45	1.55	1.64	1.73	1.82
12	0.83	1.00	1.08	1.17	1.25	1.33	1.42	1.50	1.58	1.67
13	0.77	0.92	1.00	1.08	1.15	1.23	1.31	1.38	1.46	1.54
14	0.71	0.86	0.93	1.00	1.07	1.14	1.21	1.29	1.36	1.43
15	0.67	0.80	0.87	0.93	1.00	1.07	1.13	1.20	1.27	1.33
16	0.63	0.75	0.81	0.88	0.94	1.00	1.06	1.13	1.19	1.25
17	0.59	0.71	0.76	0.82	0.88	0.94	1.00	1.06	1.12	1.18
18	0.56	0.67	0.72	0.78	0.83	0.89	0.94	1.00	1.06	1.11
19	0.53	0.53	0.68	0.74	0.79	0.84	0.89	0.95	1.00	1.05
20	0.50	0.60	0.65	0.70	0.75	0.80	0.85	0.90	0.95	1.00
25	0.40	0.48	0.52	0.56	0.60	0.64	0.68	0.72	0.76	0.80
30	0.33	0.40	0.43	0.47	0.50	0.53	0.57	0.60	0.63	0.67
35	0.29	0.34	0.37	0.40	0.43	0.46	0.49	0.51	0.54	0.57
40	0.25	0.30	0.33	0.35	0.38	0.40	0.43	0.45	0.48	0.50
45	0.22	0.27	0.29	0.31	0.33	0.36	0.38	0.40	0.42	0.44
50	0.20	0.24	0.26	0.28	0.30	0.32	0.34	0.36	0.38	0.40
100	0.10	0.12	0.13	0.14	0.15	0.16	0.17	0.18	0.19	0.20

TABLE 2

Testing for Success

Size of test mailing required on a desired response rate ranging from 0.5% — 20% and a percentage error tolerance level of 0.2% — 1.0% at a confidence level of 95%.

RESPONSE RATE	ERROR TOLERANCE				
	0.2	0.3	0.4	0.5	1.0
0.5	4776	2123	1194	764	↑
0.6	5725	2545	1431	916	↑
0.7	6672	2966	1668	1068	↑
0.8	7618	3386	1905	1219	↑
0.9	8562	3805	2140	1370	↑
1.0	9504	4224	2376	1520	↑
1.5		6304	3546	2269	LESS THAN 1000
2.0		8363	4704	3011	
2.5			5850	3744	
3.0			6984	4470	
3.5			8106	5187	↓
4.0			9216	5898	↓
4.5				6601	↓
5.0				7296	↓
5.5				7983	↓
6.0				8663	
6.5				9335	1167
7.0				9999	1250
7.5					2664
8.0					2836
8.5					2986
9.0					3144
9.5					3301
10.0					3456
15.0					4896
20.0					6144

NOTE OF CAUTION:This table is designed for large lists. If testing a significant proportion of a list, adopt a less precise approach, eg. roll-out 5000

CHAPTER 5

TELEPHONE SALES

Introduction

The use of the telephone as a media for selling has become increasingly common over the past ten years and its popularity will undoubtedly increase in the future. Telemarketing is similar to Direct Mail in that both techniques involve the selling organisation contacting the prospect rather than waiting for the prospect to contact them.

The Benefits of Telemarketing

The main advantage of Telemarketing is that it is relatively cheap when compared with other methods such as Direct Mail — it does not involve the production of glossy brochures or the use of expensive advertising agencies; all that is required is a telephone and some knowledge of telephone sales.

The second point in favour of Telemarketing is that when the prospect is on the telephone, the seller has the prospect's full attention. The prospect does something physical when on the telephone to a salesperson — he or she has to hold the 'phone to their ear and, as a result, are constantly aware of the sellers presence, whereas, a travelling salesperson can easily be ignored. However, the prospect can very easily hang up on a Telemarketer whereas a standard salesperson has to be persuaded to leave an office.

With telemarketing the seller can immediately get an idea of whether the prospect is genuinely interested in the call or whether he or she would rather not be bothered. This means that time can be saved on the call. If the prospect is not interested, do not pursue the matter any further.

How To Sell Over The Phone

This section illustrates some of the techniques required when attempting to sell your product or service over the phone and includes the script used by the Telemarketing Department of Punter's Carpet Cleaners (See Chapter 4).

Telephone Manner

When a travelling salesperson walks into a prospect's office, the prospect will immediately judge that person on dress, posture, handshake and general introduction and then decide whether or not to listen to what he or she has to say. If the salesperson has a good presentation, the prospect will listen whereas if the salesperson is untidy or unenthusiatic, the prospect will be put off from listening. Over the telephone, however, the prospect is unable to make these judgements and so you must work that much harder to catch the prospect's attention. The first step towards doing this is to develop a telephone manner.

It is important to be pleasant to your prospect but, as with any other forms of sales, don't gush — it may be taken as sarcasm. Try to smile over the phone, it doesn't matter if this is your one hundred and fiftieth call and the previous on hundred and forty-nine have been rejections, if you sound depressed the prospect will not be willing to do business with you.

Introduce yourself using your first name (more on this is the next section) but beware of annoying the prospect by overdoing it. An example of this would be: "Hi, this is Dave, is Norman there?" This could be seen as being over friendly, especially if Norman didn't know a Dave, and would instantly put Norman on his guard. If Norman did know a Dave and made the mistake of taking the salesman for the other Dave, then he would feel foolish and less disposed to hear what the salesperson has to say.

An approach that is more likely to make the prospect want to listen would be for Dave, the salesperson, to ask "Could I speak to Norman Aikins please?" This then gives Norman the opportunity to decide whether or not to speak to Dave and, should he decide that he will talk to him, he will be willing to listen since he will not feel as if he has been pressured.

When actually talking, it is important that you speak clearly and intelligibly — do not mutter or mumble and make sure when pronouncing names of firms, products or organisations you say the names clearly and, if the prospect asks you to spell the name, make sure you do know how it is spelt.

Finally, when ending a conversation always ensure that you thank the prospect for his or her time whether they are interested or not. If the prospect is not interested, apologise for having disturbed them. If they are interested, however, sound enthusiastic about speaking to them again and let them know that you will not be inactive during this time. You could, for instance, tell the prospect that you will send some literature to them through the post.

The Script

When making a call, you should appear as professional as you possibly can, even if you have had no experience in telesales before. To help you achieve this you should work out a script so that you will know exactly what to say and exactly how to respond to any arguments that the prospect may put forward. The following extract gives a good example.

This method may seem laborious, but it will ensure that you are able to respond to the more common situations that arise during telesales conversations. Eventually, as you become used to your task you will be able to dispense with the script and work for yourself.

QUESTION:		Would you be interested in seeing a demonstration of the hot water injection system?	
POSSIBLE ANSWERS:	No, not at all	Tell me more about it and I might	Yes, definitely
RESPONSE:	Well do you realise that your business could only benefit from having clean carpets . . .	Very well, the hot water injection system involves . . .	Splendid! Do you think that you could give me a date and time that would suit you best . . .

Turning a "No" into a "Yes"

The good telesales representative will have the ability to convert a negative rejection from a prospect into a positive acceptance and the secret of this is to emphasise the good points of your product. If a prospect turns you down straight away you should try to pursuade them that their lives will be improved by the purchase of your product or use of your service for instance:—

Q—"Good morning; I represent Punter's Carpet Cleaners and I am ringing to find out if you would be interested in seeing a demonstration of our new carpet cleaning facility".

A—"No, I'm sorry I'm really not very interested and I don't have time".

Q—"I understand sir but, before you ring off, could I just point out that the impression a visitor to your office receives may only be improved if you allow us to treat your carpets, and, as for time, a demonstration takes a mere ten minutes so you will not be inconvenienced in that sense?"

A—"Well O.K. if you call at twelve-thirty on Tuesday the eigth I'll be able to see a demonstration then".

This is a slightly simplistic example since it is unlikely that any salesperson would be able to generate a lead this easily, although it does illustrate just how easy it is to turn a "No" into a "Yes".

Positive Answer

One of the most widely used "tricks of the trade" is the positive answer technique. This involves giving your prospect a choice in which he or she has no choice at all. Rather than saying, as an example. "Do you wish to see a demonstration?", you should say "Do you wish to see a demonstration or would you rather I sent you some literature"?

In this way, you gently direct your prospect towards giving a positive answer to your questions and this brings you closer to making a sale. To give you some idea of how to go about doing this, table 1 shows some common decisions requiring sentences that occur during sales on the left and the column on the right shows the same sentence in positive answer form:—

Table 1

Do you wish to see a demonstration?	**Do you wish to see a demonstration or shall I send you some literature**
Do you want to buy Product Y?	**Would you like to buy Product Y or product X?**
Would you buy one of our products?	**Would you buy one, two or three items?**

The Do's and Dont's of Telesales

If you are considering embarking upon a telesales drive and either yourself, of your team, is inexperienced it would be a good idea to memorise these points or, copy them out and pin them above the telephone:—

DO's —

- Always make the prospect feel as if they have the advantage;
- Always treat the prospect with respect;
- Always use a friendly telephone manner;
- Always smile over the 'phone;
- Always have a script handy in case you get stuck;
- Always make sure you can spell the names of firms, products or organisations and;
- Always speak clearly over the telephone.

DONT's —

- Never insult or humiliate the prospect;
- Never appear to be over-friendly;
- Never harrass the prospect;
- Never use closed questions and;
- Never ask questions that are too personal.

Example

The dialogue that follows is taken from Punter's Carpet Cleaner's telesales department and was recorded as a training aid for other staff members. The dialogue occurs between the Prospect (P) and the Salesperson (S).

S — Good morning, may I speak to P please.

P — Speaking

S — Hello my name is S and I represent Punter's Carpet Cleaners. I was wondering if you would be interested in seeing a demonstration of our new Hot Water Injection carpet cleaning system.

P — No, sorry I'm not

S — Well could I ask, do you know anything about this system?

P — No, I don't and, as I said, I'm not very interested.

S — Could I just point out that this may well help to increase your profitability.

P — Oh, how so?

S — By ensuring that your carpets are thoroughly clean you will improve the image of your offices no end and impress any walk—in customers.

P — Isn't that a little far fetched?

S — No, madam, not at all, and it will also save you money in the long run.

P — Go on.

S — Well, when people trample over the carpets in your office any dirt or grit that is on their shoes is deposited in the carpet fibres and, over time, will wear your carpet down. This means that you will eventually have to replace it but, if you have your carpets treated regularly, say every six months, by us, you will at least quadruple the life of your carpet. Now, in the light of this new information, would you now like a demonstration or would you rather I posted some literature on to you?

P — Well, I could spare you half an hour at eleven-fifteen on Wednesday the fourteenth.

S — That would be fine. We will send a representative to your office then and, in the meantime, I will send you some of our brochures through the post. Thankyou very much for your time. Goodbye.

P — Goodbye.

SUMMARY

- Telesales has grown quickly over the past ten years;
- Telesales is cheap when compared with other sales media;
- Telesales ensures the full attention of the prospect;
- With telesales, the seller can instantly tell whether the prospect is genuinely interested;
- The salesperson should have a good telephone manner;
- The salesperson should not gush or be too pushy;
- The salesperson should always use a script as a guide;

- If the salesperson can change a "no" into a "yes" they will stand a good chance of increasing their sales or leads;
- The use of the positive answer technique will also increase the chances of making a sale.

REFERENCES AND FURTHER READING

Marks, P. *The Telephone Marketing Book*. Business Books Ltd.

Patten, D. *Successful Marketing for the Small Business*. Kogan Page.

REFERENCE ADDRESSES

1. British Direct Marketing Association
   Grosvenor Gardens House
   London
   SW1W 0BS
   Tel. 071 630 7322
2. Datapro Research Group (Directory Suppliers)
   McGraw—Hill House
   Maidenhead
   Berks
   SL6 2QL
   Tel. (0628) 773628

CHAPTER 6

ADVERTISING

Introduction:—

Advertising is a vital investment for those marketing based firms that wish to progress in their fields. Advertising is not an irksome expense but an invaluable investment. Where to advertise depends on the location of the company and the type of product or service being marketed. This section gives guidance on where and how to advertise.

The role of advertising must be distinguished from Public Relations (PR) in that:—

- PR is the devlopment of the organisation's image in the eyes of the public whereas;
- ADVERTISING is a means of increasing sales through the media.

Where will the selling firm find new customers? How will it announce that the firm has moved to new prestigious premises? Advertising can accomplish these and many other issues.

The objective of advertising is to make potential buyers respond more favourably to the firm's offerings, and seeks to do this by providing information and attempting to modify desire by supplying reasons for preferring their firm's particular product(s) (1). The **constructive** function of advertising is to explain the product or service and its availability, its **combative** function is to undermine the prospect's loyalty to other products and services.

Advertising is an important part of a firm's selling effort and needs to be planned and conducted professionally. The campaign should be kept under constant review and various media tried if only to discover which is the most effective in terms of cost and effort. Whilst the foremost task will be to promote a product or a service, to create a favourable impression of the firm and to counter competition, there are many other tasks that the successful advertisement can accomplish. They can be listed as:—

- Tell potential buyers about a new product and encourage them to buy it.
- Maintain sales by keeping the product(s) in the public eye.
- Create new markets or revolutionise existing ones.
- Stimulate new interest in an existing product by announcing a modification/improvement.
- Boost sales, by promoting a special offer.
- Sell direct. 'Off the peg' selling is found in most newspapers and magazines and covers a vast range of offerings.
- Encourage people to send for information, samples or a brochure.
- Encourage stockists.
- Create goodwill and company image through corporate advertising.
- Educate. The Government is the main advertiser in the field of educational and public interest matters; e.g. in its road safety campaign, Health and Education Council's efforts to get people to take more exercise, give up smoking etc.
- Invite job applicants.
- Sell to the trade by advertising, not to the general public but to members of specific trades or professions.

Advertising Media

Reference has been made to using a mix of advertising media to ensure that the market place is covered effectively. The following methods, not in any order of preference, are summarised with a note on some of the advantages and disadvantages of each.

Cinema — Inside a cinema auditorium the advertiser has a captive audience. This method is inexpensive and relevant to the local shops, businesses, hotels and restaurants.

Parking Meters — there are 35,000 parking meters in the UK used by more than 5 million motorists each week. For firms wishing to reach the motorist, advertising here could be effective. The local authority will supply details, and costs are relatively low.

Point of Sale — having attracted customers to a retail shop or store it is more sensible to remind them about a firm's product and why they should buy it. Reprints of advertisements made into counter cards and the use of posters, signs and attractively presented samples can stimulate sales.

Suppliers will often provide indoor point of sale displays.

Promotional Gifts — carrying the firm's name in the form of pens, carrier bags, key rings and book matches are a method used by many big firms.

Sandwich Boards — this can be a useful method of advertising a shop or business located in a side street. It is necessary to check with the local authority first in case permission is required.

Transport Advertising — taxis, buses and tube trains carry advertising. The message on the outside of moving vehicles will be short but more detail can be included on adverts placed inside tubes and buses. For local businesses this method can provide a low cost means of communicating with prospects.

Theatre Programmes — theatre programmes can be effectively used in promoting a firm and its offerings, in the same way as in PR.

Telephone Kiosks — telephone kiosks provide another source for local businesses. Taxi firms could find this source particularly useful at some sites.

Book Marks — paper book marks can be used and can possibly be given to local libraries to distribute.

Other Methods — amongst the 'high flying' methods of promoting a firm's product or for promoting a sale may be included; hot air balloons, tethered balloons and aerial advertising by using a plane to tow a message over a seaside resort or other area providing a large audience.

Radio — this can provide a cost effective method for communicating with customers. There are more than 40 commercial radio stations in the UK. The use of radio in the UK is much lower than in the US and Canada and its use here will inevitably grow over the next few years.

Amongst the benefits of radio advertising can be included immediacy, one of its strongest advantages. Economy is another benefit; a 30 second broadcast can be bought for as little as £10 although prices rise significantly for peak-time transmissions. Production costs are generally low and the total costs are favourable when compared with television. Radio audiences can be very receptive and advertisers can capitalise on this fact; the well known and friendly voice of a broadcaster can be very persuasive. Radio is local and a recent survey notes that radio can develop a good 'community feeling' which provides another reason why the small business can benefit from advertising on local radio. Stations claim considerable listener loyalty, a high proportion of listeners follow one station and many of them have direct contact through 'phone-ins', charity and outside broadcasts. A good attitude to their favourite station provides a desirable advantage to advertisers.

One of the drawbacks of radio is the absence of visual stimuli by taking from the advertiser the advantage of exploiting the major sense of sight. Unlike press or direct mail advertisments, the listener receives nothing tangible to remind him. It cannot be assumed that listeners have a pen and paper handy to write down an advertiser's name and telephone number. In considering the use of radio, it is worthwhile accepting that fact. Whilst radio can offer significant help in promoting a firm, it should be supported by other media, for example, the press.

Television — it is not appropriate for the small firm, mainly on account of the high cost and large areas covered. Using a particular TV region may help achieve sales, although production costs can be high, most regional TV stations will offer special rates and discounts for first time advertisers.

Media — advertising media in the UK includes (1991):—

- 10 TV areas
- 16 national daily papers
- 62 provincial weekly papers
- 400+ consumer magazines

- 40 commercial radio stations
- 9 Sunday papers
- 120 provincial daily papers
- 2000+ business and trade journals

as well as directories, posters and many other methods. "British Rate and Data" (BRAD), provides information on sources of advertising media and lists them under area, price and potential audience as well as listing local 'free' publications.

Specialist Sources — there are many specialist journals covering, for example, fishing, animals, cars, aviation, etc. The radio Times provides a first class source for advertisers , being seen on average by four people per household and may be present in the house for ten days or more. Firms that have a clearly defined advertising objective have a marked competitive advantage in that they can utilise the more specialised media.

Budgeting and Objective — Methods of determining the firm's advertising budget may vary widely. For example, some recent published data for the UK engineering industry showed that:

28% had no known basis
39% employed a fixed sum method
29% based expenditure on a % of the previous year's sales
4% used other methods

This approach makes advertising appear to be a nonentity. Most firms have a trade cycle when income drops some firms reduce advertising expenditure which tends to exaggerate the trade cycle, causing advertising to appear to be a cause rather than an affect. If this is the case, why advertise at all?

One of the problems in measuring the effectiveness of advertising arises because a firm's goals are not made explicit. What are they attempting to achieve with an advertising campaign? The answer to this question needs to be clearly understood and stated by the advertiser. Is the campaign designed to accent one or all of the objectives indicated by the simple diagram below?

(Unawareness — Awareness — Comprehension — Conviction — Action)

Some well known companies advertise in 'bursts', ie. advertising their product by building up to a level considered suitable and then stopping. After a period the process is repeated; firms use a 'drip' method whereby a constant and steady flow of advertising appears over the year. Which is the correct approach is debatable, possibly nobody knows but a paper worthwhile reading for background information on measuring advertising response was written by McDonald (2) who suggested that advertising is so interacted with the rest of the marketing mix that it cannot be measured independently.

The methods of advertising, and background to the American advertising industry , is given in Vance Packard's book "Hidden Persuaders".

The high cost of employing people means that some firms whose customers are irregular buyers have found it more cost effective to reduce the number of calls made by sales people and spend more on effective advertising, thus increasing the use of indirect communication with some customers in order to reduce overall selling costs, although the person may be necessary to close the sale at the final stage.

Those firms wanting their business to grow, or just survive, need to promote themselves. In these competitive times, buyers have plenty of choice and need to be frequently reminded of who and where the firm is and what it is offering. Advertising can be a good investment not just an expense, and it needs to be part of the firm's budget, not something to be done when it can be afforded.

Low Cost Advertising — it is recommended that the organisation should try a 'do it yourself' approach initially. This is recommended as a sound course to pursue before employing an agency, so that the organisation can brief an agency more fully in the light of its first experiments and results.

A firm can increase the effectiveness of its advertising by employing an agency. By considering the basics, however, the smaller firms may experiment themselves so that later they will have some yardsticks against which to judge any agency which they may be considering engaging. Setting advertising objectives is the first important consideration. Possible objectives are as follows:—

- sell the firm's product or service quickly and efficiently
- obtain new customers
- persuade regular customers to buy more
- get new sales leads
- attract dealer support and
- inform more buyers of who you are and what it is that you do.

The next stage is to clearly set down the target audiences in detail. Who is most likely to buy the firm's offerings? For domestic customers, are they men, women, or children? Which socio-economic group or income bracket? If marketing to other firms, which type, what size? To whom in the business will the offerings be made and where are these customers located?

Benefits — the other main consideration concerns those benefits to be advertised. The buyer wants to know "What's in it for me"? Those adverts which effectively stress benefits will have a greater pulling power than those which do not. In order to achieve this, the selling company needs to research those factors which will motivate prospects. Identification of such factors can be accomplished by asking questions such as — Is the firm's product and service unique? Do prospects seek convenience, beauty, good health, happiness, status and so on? Instead of listing technical features of the product, the advertiser is advised to translate most of these features into easily understood benefits.

The steps in advertising (persuasion) process can be summarised as:

Hints About Low-Cost Advertising

Because your firm will not be using a professional advertisaing agency you will not have access to many of the facilities that such a firm would be able to use. However, this does not prevent your organisation from using some of the basic techniques that the professionals use. These basics are summarised in the "do's and dont's" below:—

DO's —
- Use an easy to read typeface
- Include pictures — preferably cartoons
- Include humour in your ads — it makes them more memorable
- Word the advert in such a way as to make the reader believe that they need your product.

DON'Ts —
- Don't humiliate the reader
- Don't baffle the reader with in-depth detail

- Don't ever include disparaging comments about a competitor in the text
- Never use an advert that is boring, dull or unimaginative and
- Never use an advert that has obviously been copied from another source.

Compare and contrast the two adverts shown below:
Diagram 1 should give you some ideas on how to do it whilst Diagram 2 shows you how not to do it.

Diagram 1.

Diagram 2.

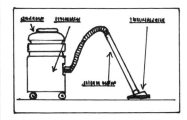

The differences are obvious. Diagram 1 tells the reader exactly what the service is, gives details on how the firm can be contacted, includes information about the free offer and there is a touch of humour in the cartoon.

Diagram 2, however, gives no details of any offers, or of how to contact the firm whilst the reader is left puzzled by the unexplained words "Hot Water Injection System" and the poorly reproduced technical diagram. The poor quality of Diagram 2 has been exaggerated. It is doubtful if anybody could produce an advert this bad!

Positioning

The positioning of outdoor advertising is all important because if the public does not see your advert, they will not know that you exist and the expenditure will be wasted.

An advert such as Diagram 1 above would be just as effective on a poster or sandwich board as in a newspaper or magazine with one or two modifications, for instance, the inclusion of a large arrow directing passers by to your offices or showroom.

Diagram 3

This could then be pasted to a sandwich board and placed on a corner nearby, as Punter's have done in Hometon.

Placing a sign on a main road will ensure that the maximum number of people will see the advertisement.

Another method of outdoor advertising involves saturating a small area such as a town centre, by pasting "Flysheets" on any available space, for instance, temporary wooden panels erected by construction companies (note that it is advisable to get permission first and this may involve a financial arrangement). The stages in advertising are as follows:

PRESENTATION

ATTENTION

COMPREHENSION

GETTING THE RECEIVER TO YIELD (COMPLY)

ENSURING RETENTION OF THE MESSAGE

INDUCING DESIRED BEHAVIOUR

A good advertising agency will assist in reinforcing all these stages and will be able to measure and monitor them using appropriate techniques and making changes where necessary in order to increase the effectiveness of any stages requiring modification.

Agencies

Firms contemplating hiring an agency or changing their existing agency, need to devote some time and thought to the main factors involved since it can cost a great deal of money. A poor decision may even create problems for the other marketing functions. Choosing one of the big name agencies may not be appropriate for some firms, rather they should seek assistance from an agency who can demonstrate a sound knowledge, understanding and contacts within the seller's particular industry. There are thousands of advertising agencies in the UK. A firm wishing to employ a local agency could consult Yellow Pages, unless based in London. The quarterly Brad Advertiser and Agency List gives details of agencies and some of their clients as well as listing clients under agency headings and offers a section on regional advertising. The publishers of Campaign produce a directory of the larger agencies called Portfolio. This publication gives detail about the agency's billing, clients and personnel and an indication of the agency's expertise in any particular medium. Another reference book available at many libraries is the Advertisers' Annual which cross references agencies by client and companies by agency. The UK Marketing Handbook also lists advertising agencies and specialist agencies. Other organisations will provide help in short listing, for example, The Advertising Agency Register, for a fee and, a suitable brief, will shortlist agencies from many of their books. They also offer a short video on each of the shortlisted agencies and detailed information about them including a sample of press advertisements. The same organisation also runs a Public Relations Register offering a service to companies trying to select a PR agent.

Assistance and Costs

Further help is available from the Institute of Practitioners in Advertising (I.P.A) (4). A firm supplying details about their needs can obtain, from this source, a shortlist (free of charge) under their Confidential Agency Recommendation Service. The recommendations are obtained through the IPA's 260 member agencies responsible for 80% of total advertising by value. Firms seeking an agency should research carefully prior to making a selection. However some of the more important factors in making a decision will be discussed in more detail.

Agencies range in size and scope from a 'one-man-band' copy writer to the large 'full service' agencies which deal with everything from market research to media-buying, but they can be expensive. The size of an agency is usually quoted in terms of total billings, the total of all the agency's clients costs in advertising, most of which goes to the media where the clients advertise. The small client may not receive the close attention and help that is given to the bigger and more lucrative client, and it is necessary therefore for a firm seeking an agency to set down clearly the skills required to fulfil its particular needs.

The major cost in advertising is the cost of the advertising space, whether it be on TV, the press, posters and so on. Obtaining a good media price negotiator is therefore a most important exercise. Agencies specialising in particular geographical locations or industrial sectors may be able to provide more buying power with local and regional newspapers or specialist magazines.

Many agencies take 15% of the client's payment to the media plus a fee related to production costs. It is in the agency's interest, because of this commision arrangement, to have the client pay the maximum for its media space. Before committing itself to an agency, the client must enquire about the method of payment in detail. It may be in the client's interest if the commission method could be altered to a straight fee approach if the quality of service provided meets its requirements.

An examination of agency listings will give details of which organisations officially 'recognise' each agency. Recognition is important because it gives an indication of the financial strength and credit-worthiness of agencies. Further, it may mean that the agency is eligible for discounts from the media that an advertiser would not be able to obtain by buying direct.

The location of the agency can be important in terms of the time that can be saved by the client's staff in travelling to meetings with the agency staff. A small regional agency which may be cheaper can be more convenient for meetings and will better understand local buyers and have good connections with local media.

It is worthwhile noting the other clients of a shortlisted agency because this will give an indication of their expertise in any sector. Agencies will specialise in a specific area such as consumer, industrial and financial advertising etc.

It is important for the selling company, seeking help from a particular agency, to arrange to meet with people with whom they will work professionally and personally. In this respect, the client company should contact the agency staff in charge of the campaign immediately, and not deal solely with a director, with whom they may have no further contact.

In dealing with agencies, the following topics should be discussed at the initial meeting(s):—

- How can the firm improve the 'sales appeal' of current brochures and technical literature?
- How can the agency provide the organisation with appropriate mailing lists and how can they be tested?
- How can conversions to sales be increased?
- How will the agency help the firm to reduce printing costs?
- How can personal sales presentations be improved?
- What is the agency's experience of direct marketing and how can the firm be assisted in overcoming the barriers to it?

Articles on 'How to make the most of advertising' were published in several parts in 1988 by the National Westminster Bank's Small Business Digest. These articles supplied free of charge cover miscellaneous information including:—

- Why advertising is important for all businesses
- How to develop the message
- What media can be used? Details of all media are given in British Rate and Data (BRAD) held at most main libraries which provide rates, circulation numbers, contacts for all magazines, radio stations and newspapers available in the UK
- Notes on cinema, consumer magazines, direct mail, editorials and local directories.

SUMMARY

- Advertising is an investment;
- Advertising should be planned and carried out professionally;

- Advertisers should use as many media as possible;
- Smaller firms should try the do it yourself method;
- Larger firms can employ an advertising agency
- Adverts should be eye-catching, humorous, bold and to-the-point;
- Adverts should not be boring, verbose, overly technical or condescending to the reader.

REFERENCES AND FURTHER READING

Packard, V. *Hidden Persuader's*. Penguin Books, 1971.

McDonald, M. *How To Sell A Service*. Wyvern Business Library.

Jefkins, F. *Advertising Made Simple*. 4th Edition. Heinemann London, 1985.

REFERENCES ADDRESSES

1. INSTITUTE OF PRACTITIONERS IN ADVERTIS-ING
   Abford House
   15 Wilton Road
   London
   SW1V 1NJ

2. CHARTERED INSTITUTE OF MARKETING
   Moor Hall
   Cookham
   Maidenhead
   Berks
   SL6 9QH   Tel. (06285) 24922

CHAPTER 7

PUBLIC RELATIONS

Introduction:—

Effective Public Relations (PR) pays dividends for any size of business and, in the long term, generates additional profit. Many large, well known companies spend much time and considerable amounts of money on the promotion of their image. If the firm has a good image in the eyes of the public the firm is seen as being trustworthy and, when the public, customers, suppliers, bankers and the community in general understand the scope, capabilities and soundness of the firm, they develop a greater confidence in doing business with it.

Many small firms find Public Relations somewhat daunting since they believe it to be the province of big organisations who will be able to achieve good Public Relations through high quality advertising. This misconception confuses the roles of PR and advertising. The latter is a means of stimulating sales through the utilisation of buying space in newspapers and technical journals and through the use of television, radio and exhibitions. PR, however, works over a longer time period and it can give a thorough understanding of the company, its scope and its products, thus creating a climate in which the company can prosper and grow. Though both advertising and PR cost money, the latter can be a very cost effective way of getting the company noticed and remembered.

Public Relations can be defined as "the non-personal stimulation of demand for a product, service or business unit by placing significant information about it in a published medium or obtaining a favourable presentation of it on radio, television or stage without the sponsor paying for it."

In an international context, two aspects are of special importance:—

● Placing press releases with overseas media — particularly difficult for the exporter;
● Becoming a "good citizen" in the host country —particularly difficult for overseas subsidiaries, see Walsh (4).

Marketing and Size of Organisation:—

Before seeking to promote its image and make closer contact with the appropriate media, the small firm is advised to set down clearly the reasons why it is special or unique. This analysis may throw light on changes in management style, products or services and methods of operation that may become necessary. The organisation should commence by asking a number of key questions:—

● What are the organisations main strengths?
● What are its weaknesses?
● What future opportunities are expected that may increase the profitability of the enterprise?
● What major threats or dangers lie ahead and how can they be turned into opportunities?

The results of this exercise need to be summarised and given to all managers, supervisors and to the workforce. This can then become part of the Corporate Planning Process.

Opinion Influencers:—

The next step should be to list those people and organisations that can influence the attitudes and opinions of others. This list should include:—

- Past Customers;
- Present Customers;
- Future Customers;
- Key Suppliers;
- Opinion Leaders;
- Local Authority Officers;
- Educational Establishments;
- Local and Regional Newspapers
- Trade Journalists and;
- Local Radio and Television

The job of making contact with these should be given to an enthusiastic member of the firm's marketing division. After making contact, the representative should ensure that he or she is adequately prepared to answer questions from the contact, and to deal with other, unexpected questions that the contact may ask.

The Local Press

The Local Press, including the "free sheets", can be valuable allies in any PR effort since they are very often willing to publish articles about new enterprises within the region. Firms anxious to improve their PR should not be slow in approaching the press, who will be keen to publish articles concerning such things as:—

- A visit by a prestigious person;
- A new or larger order from a well known company;
- The supply of goods or services to a foriegn country;
- An innovative new product or seminar;
- An achievement by a number of the firm that drew attention to the organisation.

Writing the Article:—

It is of the upmost importance that the article captures the readers interest, otherwise it will be quickly skimmed over without the reader absorbing the information. So it is advisable to use a "hard-hitting" headline that will increase the readers expectations.

The article should then begin by stating the facts that the headline deals with. The text following this should be easy to read and should not contain too many technicalities as this will bore the reader. Don't make the article too long as the reader will become disinterested. When writing a press release such as

LOCAL COMEDIAN TAKEN TO THE CLEANERS

Well known local comedian Billy Jones was taken to the cleaners yesterday, quite literally. He was the guest of honour at the celebrity opening of the Yardgate branch of "Punters Carpet Cleaners". After the silk ribbon had been cut there was an informal lunch, attended by representatives from many local businesses and charities. After lunch the guests were entertained by Billy Jones who gave a brilliant performance.

In her short speech, Ms Roberta Punter, the Managing Director said, "I hope that the Yardgate branch will be as successful as the other branches in the region and that we will be able to offer a high standard of service in the years to come".

The photograph shows Roberta Punter (left) and Billy Jones declaring "Punters" officially open.

the one on the previous page, it is important to bear in mind the differences between advertising and PR. The use of the local press is a PR exercise, not part of an advertising campaign. Most Local Newspapers will reject articles that contain some attempt at advertising.

The inclusion of a photograph in a press article will also be of value as it will act as an "eye-catcher" and help to illustrate the text. The reader will be better able to remember the article and, hence, the organisation about which the article is written if the photograph has some points of interest or is humorous.

Radio and Television:—

An appearance on television or radio can be extremely daunting for those who have never done it before and so it is initially important that you make adequate preparation. Some of the points that should be remembered are:—

- If you are being interviewed, make sure you know the questions that you are going to be asked as this will prevent any potentially embarassing replies to difficult questions;
- Ask for a preliminary tour of the studio — this will make the technology less daunting;
- Relax during the interview and do not fidget or wriggle in your chair;
- Arrive on time. If you arrive with little time to spare before the interview, you will appear flustered or, worse still, if you are late, you may well lose the opportunity to appear at all.

Sponsorship:—

The Sponsorship of local events such as charity fund raisers, sports events, theatre productions or travelling fairs can provide excellent PR opportunities for firms.

The most common form of sponsorship is that of sports events. All of us can think of at least three international sporting events that have the name of a large organisation attached to them — "Stella Artois" Tennis Tournament, "Kellog's Milk Race" and the "Lombard R.A.C." Rally are good examples of this. The large companies can afford to pay vast sums of money to get their name attached to an event, but small companies can do a similar thing only on a smaller scale. A sports firm could supply the boots for a local football game in return for having their name appear on the team's strip, for instance.

Many small shops are able to place adverts in theatre programmes because they have provided some form of service for the cast, crew or production itself. A common example of this is furniture shops. The shop provides some furniture for the set and, in return, is given a small space in the programme.

Travelling fairs or circuses provide excellent PR opportunities for a firm. A large mention in the programme or over the tannoy is the reward for the firm that is willing to pay for the hire of the land or provide catering services for the circus or fair.

Charity :—

A firm's image in the public eye can be improved if it is seen to be making regular donations to a charitable organisation. By placing a reference to this fact on your packaging or in your advertising, the public will feel good about buying your product, "Punters", in their most recent advertising campaign, included the line:—
"Punter's will donate 12% of your fee to the Save the Children Fund."
There will be many other examples of this that you can think of yourself.

As a final point, it should be ensured that donations are made to an organisation to which the public can relate easily, preferably a large one such as "Save the Children" or "The World Wide Fund for Nature". If Punters had made their donations to "The Flooring Textile Fitters Benevolent Fund". their campaign may not have been as successful as it was.

Speaking :—

Public speaking is another means of improving PR for your organisation with very little effort. If you are asked to speak at, say, a dinner, do not turn the opportunity down. An introduction that names your firm could well bring you the attention to someone that may be looking for services such as those offered by your firm, but who has never heard of your company before. The situations where this is most likely to occur are after-dinner speeches such as those given after "Round-Table" or Masonic dinners.

Conclusion :—

PR opportunities are all about you — take them!

SUMMARY

- Effective PR pays dividends for a business or organisation of any size;
- PR works over a larger time period than advertising and provides the customer with a more thorough knowledge of the firm;
- PR tends to be more cost effective than advertising;
- There are many media that can be used in order to improve a firms PR;
- Firms and organisations should be constantly aware of the need to find these PR opportunities and use them effectively;
- Any organisation that does not have an effective Public Relations campaign is missing out on a initial means of increasing its market standing.

REFERENCES AND FURTHER READING

Jefkins, F. *Public Relations For Your Own Business.* Mercury Paperbacks.

Bland, M. *Be Your Own P.R. Man and Practical P.R. for the Small Business.* Kogan Page.

Small Business Digest (Vol. 22) July 1986. National Westminster Bank.

Walsh, L.S. *International Marketing.* MacDonald and Evans. 1981.

CHAPTER 8

EXHIBITIONS

Introduction:—

The objective of a market orientated company when taking part in an exhibition should be to display its product to the largest number of potential buyers and to seek prospects that can be followed up later. If a new or modified product, or range of products can be shown, so much the better. Choosing the type of exhibition and its location are important considerations, in view of the many possibilities available.

In evaluating an exhibition it is necessary to study the type of visitor attending and the methods of attracting them, before, during and after the exhibition, rather than the numbers of people attending.

Whilst there are many stories about small businesses exhibiting their product(s) at the right time and place and, in this way, starting on the path to making a fortune, there are many who query the benefits to be derived from this method of contacting customers. Cost comparisons of the various media for contacting customers reveal that exhibitions can be very costly — much more expensive than personal selling. Many exhibitors have found that the cost and time would have been better spent in pursuing the more traditional methods. Cunningham and White (1) comment, with examples, on the cost effectiveness of industrial marketing in their book "Role of Exhibitions in Industrial Marketing". Nevertheless, exhibitions are growing at a considerable rate and can provide a good method of generating sales and can lead to increased turnover and profitability, provided that some fundamental thinking is applied. The reasons given by many companies for exhibiting regularly include the propositions that "they must be there" or that they need to "fly the flag"; however, they may be mistaken. Those members of the Sales or Marketing function who regard exhibitions as a means of providing an annual outing for sales staff that is made more enjoyable by entertaining old customers, should be advised that there are alternative methods, less costly and more productive.

Setting Up an Exhibition

Once your firm had decided that it will take part in an exhibition or put on an exhibition itself there are several crucial factors that must be considered. These are:—

- Location(if the company is putting on the exhibition)
- Type of stand to be used
- Size of stand to be used
- Which exhibits are to be put on display
- How many staff will be on the stand and
- Will the display contain any other media.

Location

If your firm is actually putting on the exhibition rather than simply taking part in it then you must decide where to hold the exhibition and this is, really, all a matter of common sense — a zoo would hardly be a suitable venue for an animal rights exhibition yet it would be perfect for an exhibition concerning conservation.

There must be adequate transport to the town that you choose so somewhere with a motorway nearby and a large mainline railway station would be suitable. The venue must have an adequate number of parking spaces and must be large enough to hold visitors comfortably and allow them to move about without difficulty. So, to ensure this, you should try to find out how many visitors will be attending your exhibition (this is providing that it is a trade or private function rather than a public one).

The venue must be warm and comfortable otherwise, if your guests are cold, they will not be able to concentrate on the matter in hand.

As a final point, it may be worthwhile noting that an exhibition that takes place in an area relating to the subject of the exhibition for instance a Clothing exhibition being held in Manchester or a Beer exhibition in Burton-on-Trent or a Textiles exhibition in Leeds will have great appeal.

Type of Stand:—

There are two basic types of stand used at exhibitions — The Shell Stand (Diagram 1) and the Display Stand (Diagram 2). Most of the larger exhibitions use the shell stand whereas the ordinary display stand is usually found in the smaller venues.

Both stand types have advantages: the shell stand is more costly, but gives your display a distinctively up-market

Diagram 1

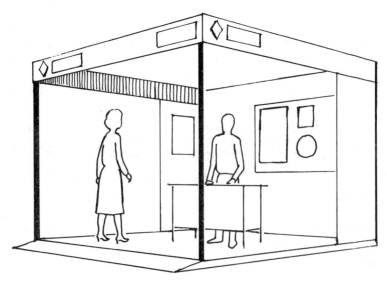

Diagram 2

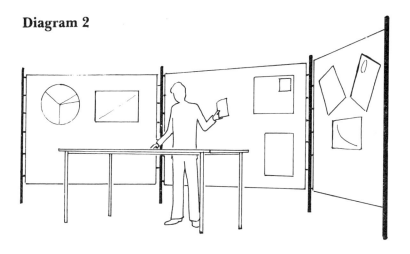

appearance. The display stand however, is easily portable and realtively cheap.

Display Design

Display design is all important — it could make or break the exhibition for you. All displays are limited by certain regulations — fire, load-bearing capacity of the floor and exhibit size being the main ones. For this reason, it is advisable to check with the exhibition organisers exactly what is allowable. For example, if you manufacture aeroplane engines it would be no easy task to get a sample of your product into a hall and display it without having to inconvenience other exhibitors, plus the fact that the floor probably would not be able to hold the weight of one of your engines. However, scale models of the engine that you produce would be perfectly acceptable.

Once you have cleared your display with the organisers, you can begin to concentrate on the layout of your stand and its position within the venue. The display must be attractive — lots of bright colours in such things as charts or graphs or possibly something that will arouse the curiosity of passers-by, such as an example of your product. If your organisation offers a service rather than manufacturing a product, you could display some of the tools used in the service.

Giving away lots of free gifts will ensure that the name of your organisation is remembered even after the prospect has left your stand — pamphlets, bookmarks, badges and carrier bags are just a few examples of low-cost, effective, free gifts.

You must ensure that visitors can get into the display without having to struggle. If they find it difficult to get in, they will not struggle on: they will leave.

The sign above the stand should be bright and attractive and should be worded in such a way as to attract visitors. The inclusion of words "NEW" or "FREE" are guaranteed to attract prospects.

Staffing the Stand

You should ensure that your stand has sales people working on it at all times for two very good reasons: firstly, it will help prevent thefts from your stand (it does happen) and, secondly, it will ensure that no prospect can escape without having been given a full briefing about your product or service.

Use trained salespeople on your stand if at all possible as this will make the display appear to be all the more professional. If this cannot be arranged, then you should try and train some of your staff to do the job. They should follow some of the following points:—

- Be pleasant, but don't gush
- Do not pressure the prospects into commiting themselves
- Spend most of the time with the prospects that are genuinely interested in your product or service
- Answer questions truthfully — if you don't know the answer,pass the prospect on to someone who does and
- Always ask "open" questions that will direct the customer towards responding to you in a positive way.

There should always be enough staff on the stand to keep it operating efficiently throughout the exhibition because, if you do not, and one team member slopes off for a quick smoke, things could easily become difficult for the remaining team members. If, however, that team member can get someone to cover for them, there should be no problem.

Publicity

It is very important that you advertise your presence at the exhibition before the actual event takes place because it is quite possible that some visitors will come to see your stand specifically. If the exhibition is a public event, then adverts in the local newspaper that serves the region in which the event is to be held and adverts placed in your own local newspaper should be adequate.

If you are attending a trade exhibition rather than a public or private one then similar adverts should be placed in trade journals that are related to the field of business. The advert shown in Diagram 3 appeared in the trade journals of the Carpet Cleaning Industry, the Carpet Manufacturing

Diagram 3

Industry, the Detergent Industries and the Carpet Cleaning Industry. Because the "Hot Water Injection System" was an innovative product that was not very well known, many firms were attracted by this advert and enquiries into Punter's services rose by 25% whilst actual sales rose by 15%.

Information Gathering

Exhibitions are not only a means of showing off your products or services — they can also be used to gain useful information about competitors. When a member of your team has a spare moment, ask him or her to go over to a rival stand. Posing as a visitor, and ask some innocent questions ("How much is this? How does it work? How well does it perform?) In this way you will be able to gain some idea about the competition's strength and weaknesses. This is not sneaky or underhanded — your competitors are doing it to you as well.

Using an Exhibition Specialist

It is suggested that, as a marketing tool, exhibitions can, and should be, exciting, challenging and rewarding. Many companies, however, fail to understand this and thus fail to exploit the potential fully. According to Exhibition Specialists:—

- A good exhibition stand needs to catch the visitor's eye within seconds.
- The need to use bold, bright colours, big letters, good graphs, videos, proper furniture, and lighting are vital in arresting customers.

Although a good display and quality literature will draw customers, too much could prove to be a disadvantage. Sending out too many "messages" may confuse the visitors: sending out too few messages may cause the exhibitor to be ignored by visitors.

- It is suggested that, unless the exhibitor actually has, within the company, someone who can not only do his or her own job, but also act as a stand designer, the company should hire the services of an experienced exhibition design consultant.
  This will be costly, but paying for an injection of professionalism will show benefits and the final rewards will be more profitable.

- A good exhibition design consultancy will do more than supply a good stand designer. They will also:—
- Research on exhibition dates for the exhibitor's products;
- Select the most appropriate exhibition(s);
- Negotiate stand size and space;
- Brief exhibition staff and;
- Help and communicate with visitors before and after the event.

SUMMARY

- Exhibitions provide a means of displaying a product and service;
- Although costly, the benefits, of exhibitions normally outweigh the initial investment.
- The location of an exhibition should be easy to find, it should have adequate transport facilities and should reflect the theme of the exhibitions;
- The venue should be of a suitable size, should have adequate parking and should be warm and comfortable;
- A shell stand or a display stand can be used in an exhibition;
- A display should comply to regulations, be attractive to visitors and have lots of free promotional gifts and literature;
- Make sure a display has plenty of staff on board;
- Any display or exhibition should be publicised;

- Using a professional exhibition designer will cost a lot but will add professionalism to the display.

REFERENCES AND FURTHER READING

Cunningham, M and White, J. *The Role of Exhibitions in Industrial Marketing*. The Chartered Institute of Marketing. Summer 1974.

Patten, D. *Successful Marketing*. Daily Telegraph Guides. Kogan Page Ltd.

Jefkins, K. *Introduction to Marketing, Advertising and Public Relations*. Macmillan. 1982.

REFERENCE ADDRESSES

1. Silver Collins Limited
   Exhibition Organiser
   148—150 Curtain Road
   LONDON
   EC2 3AR   Tel. 071–729 0677

2. Expo—World
   Graphite Display Systems
   161 Yately Street
   Westminster Industrial Estate
   LONDON
   SE18 5TA

3. The Exhibition and Marketing Manager
   Langfords International Exhibitions
   (Promotional Gift Suppliers)
   Rigeland House
   165 Dyke Road
   HOVE
   East Sussex
   BN3 ITL   Tel. 0273–206722

4. Display World
   354 Baring Road
   LONDON
   SE12 ODU   Tel. 071–857 5505

CHAPTER 9

PERSONAL SELLING

Introduction:—

Most orgainsations have, at one time or another, been visited by a professional salesperson. These people are employed by the selling company to promote their product and to generate both sales and sales leads through direct contact with the prospect.

It is vital that this form of marketing is utilised by any firm that intends to have its product recognised by the maximum number of prospects otherwise it will be missing out on a great number of potential sales.

The aim of this chapter, then, is to give the non-professional salesperson some idea of how to go about selling their product directly to the prospect.

Why use Personal Selling?

The main reason for using Personal Selling techniques is that they bring the prospect into direct contact with the product whether through demonstration, audio-visual presentation or brochures that the salesperson may carry. This direct contact means that you may be able to make a sale immediately or, at the very least, generate a new sales lead.

During a session of face-to-face sales, you are able to judge exactly how well you are doing be the reactions of the prospect, both vocally and by his or her "body language". This means that you can tell exactly how far you need to push your sales pitch or whether you should continue at all.

One of the main effects of personal sales is to give the prospect an impression — an image that he or she will constantly associate with your organisation. The significance of this is that the image of the salesperson can make or break a sale.

Image

The most important thing to remember here is that you must appear smart but not ostentatious. No self-respecting business man would buy from someone wearing jeans and a T-shirt but, nor would they buy from a man wearing a big fur coat who is dripping in jewellery.

Wear a suit wherever possible and try to co-ordinate your outfit. It is important to appear sincere and a person that wears bright clashing colours when trying to sell a product cannot be taken seriously.

Preparation

It is extremely important that you research into the backgound of your prospect in order that you will be able to give a presentation that the prospect can directly relate to. Try to find out in advance such things as:—

- Number of employees;
- Working hours;
- Amount of your product (or similar product) that is used;
- Annual turnover of prospect organisation and;
- The names of some of those in key positions within the prospect organisation;

These facts, and many others that you can dig up, will give you a firm basis upon which to hold a conversation. The result of this is that you will be able to talk fluently with the prospect about his or her field and the prospect will feel as if you may be worth buying from.

Another advantage of having information such as this to hand is that you will be able to illustrate any points that you may wish to make much more clearly. For example, compare the two statements below — the first from a salesperson who has not done adequate research and the second from someone who has:—

1. "By using our product, you will reduce the number of times you need to clean your machinery by two thirds."
2. "By using our product, you will only have to strip down to clean your machinery once every six months rather than every two months as you have to at the moment. This represents a saving of at least fifteen thousand pounds per annum which can't be bad".

The second example is both much more detailed and much more personal. The prospect is able to relate the information directly to their organisation whilst the touch of humour at the end makes the entire sales pitch seem much more human and much less calculated.

The Introduction

The most effective introduction is a firm handshake. This will affirm your status as a salesperson who is both confident within themselves and with their product. Do not talk down to the prospect! If you treat the prospect as someone who is "lower" than yourself then there is no way that he or she will buy from you. Try to appear to be on equal basis with the prospect and remember to be both positive and pleasant. Most people enjoy doing business with a person who is nice to talk to and who has a positive attitude towards their work, their product and their organisation.

On the other hand, do not humble yourself before the prospect — this will only serve to make you appear both silly and ineffective and, as a result, you would be unlikely to make a sale.

The Sales Pitch

Once all of the introductions have been completed, it is now your responsibility to persuade the prospect to buy your product. To do this, you will use your "sales pitch". This is your own, personal, style of selling which you will have planned out before setting out on your camapaign and which will develop as you visit more and more potential clients.

When planning your sales pitch, it is important that you remember one or two important do's and dont's:

DO's
- Always appear sincere;
- Always use demonstrations or audio-visual presentations
- Always respect the prospect as an equal and;
- Always speak clearly and sound interested.

DONT's
- Never lie;
- Never humiliate the prospect;
- Never appear to be overly eager or too excitable;
- Never try to pressure the prospect into buying and;
- Never try to frighten the prospect into buying.

Demonstrations

Demonstrations are always useful during a presentation as these will give the prospect a definite idea of how your product will benefit them. There are four main forms of demonstration that can be used in this situation — the "hands-on" demonstration, the model demonstration, the audio-visual demonstration or, in the case of services rather than actual products, the graphic demonstration.

The Hands-on Demonstration

If your product is small enough to be carried easily then it would be well worth your while taking a sample along to any face-to-face sales demonstration. This means that the prospect will be able to have some actual physical contact with the product and will be able to decide whether or not it is a product worth buying.

The Model Demonstration

If your product is too large to take to a demonstration then you would be well advised to employ a professional model maker to create a scaled-down model of your product that can be carried easily. This will have the same effect as the hands-on demonstration in that the prospect will be able to visualise the product being used within his or her organisation.

The Audio-Visual Presentation

Another very common method of giving a demonstration is on either video or through projected slides, both of which can be prepared by professional organisations. The disadvantage of this method is that it does involve carrying your own T.V. and Video Recorder or Slide Projector with you. If you were to ask the prospect if you could use theirs, it would appear that you were unprepared.

The Graphic Demonstration

This is more common in situations where a service, rather than a product, is being offered to a prospect. The graphic demonstration involves hiring a professional graphic artist to draw up graphs, pie charts and histograms that represent various data that your organisation will provide. The sort of things that could be included on such charts are:—

- Profit increase of an organisation through using your service;
- Increased efficiency through the use of your product or service;
- Decreased financial expenditure by a company using your service or product.

There are two very important rules to bear in mind when gathering or presenting this information:—

1 — don't make it up — if you concoct some false figures and present them and are later found out, the reputation of your organisationwould be sorely damaged.

2 — get permission — if you use the data that pertains to a company that has used your service, get permission from that company otherwise your organisation may be in trouble.

Questions

Once you have given your presentation you should allow the prospect to ask you some questions. As a memeber of the selling organisation you should be able to answer any questions that the prospect may ask (and in any case, as a salesperson, it is your responsibility to know the answers to any questions that may arise).

However, it is likely that you will get a question that you are unable to answer. In this situation you must remember not to try to lie your way out of the situation — this will only make you look silly and give the prospect the idea that you are unprofessional and your organisation is untrustworthy. It is a much safer approach to admit that you do not know however, do not let this stop you. You should use your own portable 'phone or the prospect's phone to call your organisation and get the information that he or she wants. Deal with it in a similar way to this:—

"I'm sorry Mr Jones, but I don't actually have that information with me at the moment but, if I could use you 'phone for a moment I could easily find out for you".

Always remember that, during a presentation, honesty is the best policy.

How well is your Sales Pitch going

During your sales presentation you should look for various

signals that the prospect will give out, usually in the form of questions, that serve to provide you with some idea of how well you are doing. There are both positive and negative buying indicators and the professional salesperson should be able to detect these.

Positive Indicators

These are questions that indicate that the prospect is interested. They are usually said in a cheery, interested tone and will relate directly to your product. Some examples would be:—

- "Are there any concessions for large orders?"
- "How often does your maintenance team call in?"
- "Does this include the free offer?"

After a while you will get the hang of picking up on these indicators and using them to your advantage.

Negative Indicators

Negative indicators show the salesperson that the prospect is either not at all interested or needs some further gentle persuasion. Examples of negative indicators are:—

- "We really can't afford it"
- "We don't have enough space"
- "We're happy with the one we've got"

These negative responses can be turned into positive advantages by the professional salesperson. In order to do this you should use this negativity as a cue to highlight the positive features of the product. The responses, then, to the previous questions should be:—

- "But ours is only half the price of the one you have already"
- "Our product can be wall mounted in order to keep it out of the way"

- "Ah yes, but the one you have already is outmoded and all of your competitors are buying our new, updated model."

Again, as with question answering, be truthful — if you lie you may not be able to fulfil your promises and you will be responsible for bringing your organisation into disrepute.

Closing the Sale

Once you have delivered your presentation and dispelled any objections raised by the prospect you must close the sale. This involves gently forcing the prospect into buying from you without the prospect realising. This usually involves giving the prospect a choice which leaves them no choice at all.

The most commonly used technique is that of narrowing down the prospect's objections to only one or two and then disposing of them. You could say:—

"So, if we give you a blue one and make the flaps larger you will buy?"

The prospect then has no reason why he or she should not buy your product and you have made a sale.

Another means of closing your sale (or increasing your order) known as the the "either/or" close, is to ask the prospect:—

"Would you like one or two?"

The prospect is forced into making an order by your giving him or her no choice. Of course, you may well get a prospect who will say "Well, I'm sorry but I have no intention of placing an order with you so that question is irrelevant". Should this occur, ask your prospect to list his objections and then deal with them one by one.

Should you be asked a question about your product, rather than give a straight yes or no answer ask, "do you want to buy it if it does?" If the prospect says "No" then they will appear ignorant for asking pointless questions. In order to avoid this they will say "Yes". This is sometime referred to as the 'Sharp angle close'.

After the Sale

It is always important that you follow up after making a sale. This means that the prospect (now a client) does not feel forgotten about. Before you leave their office, make out two copies of their order — one for them to keep and one for yourself. As soon as you return to base, send a letter of confirmation to your client. However do not send it so soon as to have it land on your clients desk the very next morning. Instead, send it so that it will arrive midway between the time they placed their order with you and the delivery date.

If you follow the guidelines given in this chapter and consult some of the further reading recommended later, the information that you have gained will stand you in good stead when it comes to dealing face-to-face with a prospect.

SUMMARY

- Every firm should utilise personal selling;
- Personal Selling brings the prospect into direct contact with the product;
- During face-to-face sales, you can judge your prospect and see his or her reactions;
- Always present a sincere but approachable image to a prospect;
- Take care over your appearance/hygiene! "Look good — feel good"
- Introduce yourself on the same level as your prospect; don't talk down to them but don't be overly humble;
- Deliver a sales pitch that is sincere, believable, interesting and respectful;
- Always give a demonstration of your product or service;
- Answer all questions truthfully;
- Try to turn objections into reasons for buying your product;

- Use proper closure techniques when closing any sale and;
- Always follow up any orders you may get with a letter.

REFERENCES AND FURTHER READING

Patten, D. *Successful Marketing for the Small Business*. Kogan Page.

Schiffman, S. *Cold Calling Techniques That Really Work*. Wyvern Business Library.

Davies, P. *Your Total Image*. Wyvern Business Library.

Gerard, J. *How To Close Every Sale*. Wyvern Business Library.

REFERENCE ADDRESSES

1. NORTHGATE TRAINING
   Scarborough House
   29 James Street West
   Bath
   BA1 2BT
2. THE CHARTERED INSTITUTE OF MARKETING
   Moor Hall
   Maidenhead
   Berks
   SL6 9QH

CHAPTER 10

NEGOTIATION

Introduction

Most professional salespersons will have found themselves in situations that requires them to bargain with a second party, usually, in the case of sales, a prospective customer. If the salesperson has some knowledge of the skills of negotiation, he or she will have a distinct advantage over their client.

So, what is negotiation? The Oxford English Dictionary defines negotiation as "conferring (with another) with a view to compromise and agreement", and this, basically, sums it up. The negotiator's task is to disuss issues that have been raised during the negotiating process with the intention of reaching an agreement that is mutually acceptable to both parties. The negotiator's task is not to win outright and completely crush his or her opponent; negotiation has nothing to do with your own personal ego satisfaction. If you try to do this, you will no doubt fail to reach an agreement.

However, it must be remembered that, as a negotiator, you are employed to get the best deal you can for your company or organisation so, whilst you do not totally defeat your opponent, you must try to come out of the negotiations with the better deal or, at least one that suits your company more than it suits your opponent.

In order to be an effective negotiator, it is most important that you know your own personality and the personality of the person that you are going to negotiate with. This will give you some knowledge of what you do that may annoy the people you will be called upon to negotiate with. To help you achieve this, answer the following questions truthfully and then think how you may react to someone who behaves in this way:—

- Do I have any irritating habits eg. nail biting?
- Do I become angry easily?
- Do I tend to be sarcastic or facetious?
- Do I tend to try to be funny in negotiating situations?
- Am I unable to control my emotions?
- Do I feel embarrassed about asking for something to which I am entitled?

If you can answer "No" to all of these questions (and any others you may wish to ask yourself) then you are at least part of the way towards becoming an effective and successful negotiator.

Any negotiation scenario can be divided into eight basic steps and you would do well to remember these, especially since this was first developed as a professional training aid. It is used in its original form (after Kennedy, Benson and McMillan in "Managing Negotiations") and in numerous variations upon the theme. The eight basic steps are as follows:—

1 — Prepare
2 — Argue
3 — Signal
4 — Propose
5 — Package
6 — Bargain
7 — Close
8 — Agree (after Kennedy, Benson and McMillan)

These eight steps can be reduced to four key steps, as follows:-

- Prepare
- Argue
- Propose
- Agree

There is no need to follow these stages rigidly, one after the other. Rather, you should move back and forth between them and spend varying amounts of time on each one. This will lead to a lengthy, detailed and highly productive negotiation. By following the advice given in this chapter, you should be able to develop your skills to a point that gives you at least some degree of professionalism when it comes to negotiation.

Pre-negotiation Preparation

Preparation for all negotiations is of paramount importance. Any single negotiator, or team of negotiators that succeeds in getting this stage thoroughly mastered will find that their success rate in negotiations will improve dramatically.

The preparation stage is the point at which priority matters need to be sorted out, and **NOT** during the face to face negotiations. Decide upon a ranking for the issues to be raised in the negotiations and try and stick to this. When placing the issues in rank order, it is best to use the M I L system:—

1. What you **M**ust achieve
2. What you **I**ntend to achieve
3. What you would **L**ike to achieve

This will provide the team with a firm grasp of the detail of the negotiation issues and enable the team members to adapt to changing circumstances that may arise during the actual negotiations.

During preparation, a team may find it useful to have a "devil's advocate": one member who's role is to put forward contrary positions to those prepared by the rest of the team. This will help to test arguments for soundness and consistency.

KNOW YOUR OPPONENT

Research into the background of the buyer will provide the team with a distinct advantage. Firstly, it should be remembered that there are many different types of buyer, and, if the team can recognise the different characteristics of the buyer or buyers that they are dealing with, they will be able to make important steps towards motivating them to listen, and pay attention to, the sales person's presentation. Types of buyer includes:—

- The Talkative Buyer;
- The Timid Buyer;
- The Busy Buyer and;
- The Sarcastic Buyer

When dealing with a team of buyers, it is likely that you will come across several of these types.

If you can discover exactly what it is that the buyer wants, it is possible to give a presentation that contains all the benefits to the buyers and if this is presented with enthusiasm, it is possible to influence even the most hard-headed negotiator in favour of the selling company. The following research strategies are recommended:—

1. Research into the prospective buyer's background, company history, technical skills, negotiation skills and interests. This can be done informally over a meal (paid for by the selling company of course), and will pay valuable dividends, when the negotiations begin in earnest.
2. Clearly define the firm's objectives relating to the ideal settlement or to the maximum settlement that is required for both parties to reach agreement.
3. Try to find out what concessions or bargains the buyer maybe expecting to reach so that these can then be pre-empted in the presentation. For example, if you know that the buyer will be requesting special packaging, draw attention to the packaging of your product in the presentation. This may enable you to gain concessions from the buyer later in the proceedings.
4. Try to find out what concessions are being offered by competitors. This will enable you to match and possibly even better them.
5. Make sure that you know the cost to your company of any concessions you may be asked to make. This way you will be in a position to decide whether or not to allow them.
6. Find out everything you can about the financial strengths

and weaknesses of the buyer. You will then have an indication of what their limits are.

7. Try to find out the details of offers made by competitors (this is assuming that your company is not the first that the buyer has approached). The buyer may try to bluff and suggest that he or she has had offers better than the ones you have made. If you know the truth, you will be not be taken in by this.

If adequate research is carried out, and each member of the team is fully aware of the results of this research, your team will have a distinct advantage over the opposing negotiators when the time for the actual negotiations arrive.

Concessions

Throughout the negotiations, it will be necessary to make various concessions in order to reach an amicable and mutually acceptable agreement. However, it is entirely possible to use concessions to your own advantage and so it is important that several rules are followed when negotiating concessions:—

- Always know exactly what concessions you are free to make and, as has been said earlier, what they will cost you.
- Never use up all of the concessions at your disposal too early in the proceedings, this will leave you with nothing to bargain with later — a situation which could become difficult as you search desperately for new concessions.
- Always introduce concessions slowly. This will help pace you and allow your opponent to think he or she has an advantage over you, thus putting the opponent in a more relaxed mood and making them more willing to concede to some of your requests. Follow the slow concession path.

During the Negotiations

It is vitally important that the seller should pay close attention to both the words and actions of the buyer at all times throughout negotiations and, more particularly, at the beginning of the proceedings: at the onset of negotiations the buyer may well use key phrases or words that indicate that he or she may be preparing to ask for concessions.

The buyer's words should be listened to carefully and, if necessary, their true meaning interpreted. For instance, if the buyer states that "this is my limit", it may be that he or she has to consult someone in a senior position and this person may be persuaded to go beyond the limit. It is possible to tell, through the words of the buyer, how well the negotiations are proceeding. If the buyer suggests "that factor is worth considering", it could well indicate that the negotiations are going the seller's way. Similarly, when the buyer says "I wish I could but.....", it probably means "I can buy, but I need a little more convincing". This is known as signalling.

When negotiations appear to be becoming difficult, the seller should ask why? You should seek to have points justified by asking this. For instance "I understand that you will not accept the discount of 7% that we are offering rather than the 7½% for which you are asking, but could you please explain why"?

It is important that all negotiators ask questions during the proceedings and take careful note of the replies. This may provide something useful from which you can work later, particularly if you ask "open" questions that require a long answer rather than "closed" questions that require only a simple "yes" or "no" response.

The answers to questions should be written down or recorded on audio tape but there is no need to do this with any great accuracy during the early stages of negotiation as this may make negotiators timid and reluctant to say anything that they may regret later. This would get the proceedings off to a very awkward start.

There are certain points that all people, when intending to negotiate with buyers should remember:—

- Never make a buyer feel foolish, particularly by highlighting weaknesses in their argument. This will make them defensive and less willing to buy from you.

- Never become hostile in a negotiating situation, even when the opposing negotiator does. If the salesperson becomes angry, he or she will undoubtedly fail.
- If the salesperson makes a mistake, do not correct it immediately. If the buyer can point out the mistake, it may well increase his or her feeling of importance and make them feel better disposed towards the seller. Always thank them for pointing the error out.
- Do not feel annoyed if the buyer makes exaggerated claims about the offers of competitors, simply ask how these claims were achieved.
- Always stress the benefits during negotiations, for example, the benefits of making a quick decision — the prices may rise, or deliveries may be delayed by the current demand.
- Always be straight and honest — never bend the rules and act as a wheeler dealer. At the end of the day the buyer wants to have confidence in a seller that he or she trusts.
- Always aim high at the beginning of negotiations. There is no need to lower standards in order to achieve a quick solution.
- Always give sound reasons for not accepting concessions. You must justify them and not try to avoid the subject.

Finally, a word about deadlines. It can be dangerous to impose certain deadlines during negotiations as these can hinder the process. However, some deadlines can be used to give one team an advantage:—
Deadlines that may help one team are those that :—

- Force the other negotiator(s) to make a decision.
- Impose costs on the other team.
- The other negotiators do not control
- Give the team options.

Deadlines that can hinder are those that:—

- Are imposed by the team's principles.
- Are imminent.
- Remove the negotiator's discretion.
- Cannot be ignored.

If you follow these points, and use some of the "tricks of the trade" that follow, you are bound to stay on top in any negotiation.

Tricks of the Trade

In order to be an effective negotiator, it is necessary to know a few of the "tricks of the trade" that will enable you to gain a better deal for your company. These are in no way "dirty tricks". There is nothing underhand about them; they are simply a means of delaying the process, altering the situation or getting more for your efforts. The most common of these will be dealt with one by one:—

- There is no need to dive into the negotiations headlong with one huge demand: your demands can be slowly built up until you reach your intended maximum, thus making the demand more platable to the opposition. An example of this would be beginning the negotiations by demanding a 25% discount and, when your opponent asks for a concession, raising the 25% to 30%. Then, when your opponent asks for another, larger concession, raising your 30% to the 40% that was your intended target all along. In his book "Everything is negotiable", Gavin Kennedy refers to this tactic as "salami" — take small slices each time.
- You may find that your opponent is about to present a deal that you find unacceptable. Rather than flatly rejecting the deal, you can make it appear less valid by picking as many holes in it as you can the highlighting its faults, particularly those that will affect the opposing team. For instance, if the other team makes a concession

that you can forfeit, turn it against them; if you make a concession appear to be a fault, the other members of the opposing team and, ultimately, the proposition, will be thrown out altogether.

- The opponent may ask for a concession that he or she sees as being valuable but costs you very little. This can be used to gain your team concessions from the opponent — a concession with a greater value than the one that you intend to give. These smaller matters are known as 'straw issues' and can be used to gain very valuable concessions for your company.

- You may find that your opponent wishes to vary the terms that have been agreed before the negotiations began (initial price for instance), thus taking away any advantage you may have had. This can be prevented by claiming that you do not have the authority to allow such changes to be made. This will then force your opponent to revise his or her expectations to your advantage. This is referred to as the 'Limited Authority' technique.

- Once your opponents have accepted your deal, you may be able to squeeze a little more from them by telling them that they must amend the agreement slightly due to circumstances beyond your control. If your opponent wants your product badly enough, he or she will undoubtedly agree.

- It is possible to gain one final concession by reminding your opponents of the favours that you have done them. You say "I have given you 3.5% discount, better delivery services and a wider selection of colours and I think that, in return, you can give me a small increase in the size of your order", thus making the increased order size appear more palatable to your client.

- Finally, it is possible to gain many more small concessions in the deal by, firstly, finding one small point that does not suit you. Because this is only a small point, your opponent may well be willing to concede on this issue. Once this has happened you are then free to point out one other small matter and then another, and then another . . .

You must work with these ploys and fit them into the negotiations at suitable moments rather that following them strictly or carrying them out in a particular order. You would do well to assume that, since your opponent is also a professional, they will have read the same books as you and, should you go through each manoevre in order, it will be obvious to them exactly what your next move will be. Always use a little imagination in your negotiating and you can't go wrong.

For further information on this subject, the author would suggest "Everything is Negotiable" by Gavin Kennedy, "Managing Negotiations" by Kennedy, Benson and McMillan and "Give and Take" by Chester L Karras as essential reading. For more information on these and other texts concerning the intricacies of negotiations, see the Further Reading section at the end of this chapter.

Closing

Eventually the negotiations will reach a point at which you, as the seller, have gained as much as you think possible from your opponents. This is the time at which you should close the negotiations, thus preventing your opponent from making any changes or alterations that would be to the disadvantage of your organisation.

There are a few points that you should remember about closing as these enable you to gain a little more for your team:

- Just before you intend to close, you can offer some final, small concessions. For instance, you could allow the opponent a wider range of colours if they will increase their order by 15½%.

- Assuming your opponent is demanding 30% and you can only offer 20% but, other than this, the deal is to your liking, it is possible to "split the difference" by saying something along the lines of "Although we cannot agree to your demand of 30%, and we are at liberty to offer you 20%, if we split the difference at say 25%, we can finalise the deal, agreed?" Although you have lost a little on the deal, it should still be to your liking and you will retain the advantage.

- If you use the word "final", you must mean it. This can be used if you think that the opposition is trying to force a higher offer from you and if you are certain that your opposition is trying to bluff— "I can offer 20% and that is final". Never alter your offer once you have stated that it is final as this will make you appear to be weak or a "pushover".

There are two types of closing maneouvre that can be employed when closing a deal. There is the CONCESSION CLOSE and the SUMMARY CLOSE:

- In the CONCESSION CLOSE, it is necessary to offer your opponent one final, small concession that you may well have been holding back for just such a situation. Once you have offered the concession, you must make it apparent to your opponent that this is your final offer. A simple example would be" OK then, I'm willing to drop by 5% butthat is my final offer. Are we agreed"?
- With the SUMMARY CLOSE, though you are unable to gain any concessions from your opponent, you will prevent your opponent from withdrawing any concessions that he or she may have made or altering the deal in any way. You simply say "We are agreed that you will do X, Y and Z for us, and we will do A, B and C for you, is that final"?

There now follows a short summary of everything that has been discussed in this chapter. If you read this several times and commit parts of it to memory you will be able to refer back to it constantly.

SUMMARY

- We all negotiate

- As a negotiator, your objective is not to win, outright but to obtain the best deal for both parties.
- As a negotiator, you must understand both your own personality and that of the opponent.
- The four key steps in negotiation are:
  1. Preparation;
  2. Arguing;
  3. Proposing; and
  4. Bargaining.
- Prepare thoroughly for negotiations. Find out as much information as you possibly can about the opposition.
- Place issues in rank order (remember M—I—L).
- Never accept the first offer, no matter how attractive.
- Try to spot the hidden meaning in what your opponent says.
- Do not use concessions up too early in the negotiations.
- Always introduce concessions slowly; pace yourself.
- Always be aware of the concessions that you are at liberty to make and exactly what they will cost you.
- Pay close attention to the words and actions of your opponent.
- Try to ask "Open" questions rather than "Closed" ones, but always ask!
- Deadlines can help or hinder negotiations.
- Remember the "tricks of the trade" and make sure that you use them.
- Remember how to close the negotiations — when you have the deal that suits you best.
- Remember the concession and summary closes and use them!

REFERENCES AND FURTHER READING

Kennedy, G. *Everything is Negotiable*. Arrow Books.

Kennedy G, Benson J, and McMillan, J. *Managing Negotiations*. Business Books. Ltd. Hutchinson.

Karras, Chester L. *Give and Take*. Thomas Y Crowell. 10 East 53rd Street. New York.

Negotiation Journal, Harvard Law School. 500 Pound Lane. Cambridge. Mass. U.S.A.

Calero, H. *Winning The Negotiations*. Hawthorn Books. N. York

Neirenberg, G. *The Art of Negotiating*. Hawthorn Books. N. York.

APPENDIX 1

BODY LANGUAGE

Body Language, or non-verbal communication, is the subconscious use of movement and gesture to impart or exchange information, opinion and feeling. Whilst thought of by many as a relatively recent subject for scientific enquiry, the study of human gestures and actions goes back a long way. For example, Bulwer (1644) writes about "The Natural Language of the Hand...." and Austin (1806) gave a detailed account of "Rhetorical Delivery" to aid public speakers improve their impact on their audiences through emphasising certain gestures. So, the study of body language is not new.

More recently Birdwhistell (1970) has argued that more human communication takes place by the use of gestures, postures, position and distances than buy any other method. Indeed, Mehrabian (1969) found that the total impact of a message is about 7% verbal (words only), 38% vocal (tone of voice, inflection and other sounds) and 55% visual or non-verbal. The implications of such findings for the marketing function and its approaches to communication are obvious, and they will impact on decisions regarding choice of communication channel, approaches to conducting formal presentations and embarking on any negotiation process.

The analysis of body language — its interpretation and understanding — is necessarily scientific and the inclusion of a general guide to it in this text would be too simplistic. As gestures — individual and clustered together — and the contexts in which they are made are not mutually exclusive, further reading into the subject is strongly recommended.

However, some of the more common interpretations of a selection of gestures is given in the table, merely as an insight into what is, after all, a highly scientific subject.

Gesture	Possible interpretation
Running hand through hair	Suspicion, frustration, boredom
Shoulder shrug – exposed palms, hunched shoulders, raised eyebrows	Person does not know/ understand what is being said
Shaking hands – offering palm upward	Giving control
– offering palm downward	Taking control
Steepling hands	Having a confident attitude
Speaking with fingers covering mouth, thumb pressing against cheek	Speaker is being deceitful
Folded arms – fists clenched	Hostile and defensive attitude
– hands gripping biceps	Taking a firm stand
– thumbs up	Superior attitude
Mirror image of other person while both standing	Thinking alike
Generally copying the other person's gestures	Trying to gain acceptance

FURTHER READING

Pease, A. *Body Language, How to Read Others Thoughts by their Gestures* Cannel Publishing Company 1984

Morris, D. *Manwatching – A field guide to Human Behaviour* Grafton Books 1977

REFERENCES

Bulwer, J *Chirologia; or the Naturall Language of the Hand*, London (1664).

Austin, G *Chironomia; or a Treatise on Rhetorical Delivery*, London (1806)

Birdwhistell, R. L. *Kinesics and Context. Essays on Body Motion and Communication*, University of Pennsylvania (1970)

Mehrabian, A. *Tactis in Social Influence*, Prentice Hall (1969)

APPENDIX II

Glossary of Terms used in Negotiation

This glossary is not exhaustive and is intended as a guide to the most frequently used terms in the subject.

An AGREEMENT is a CONTRACT and negotiating an agreement sounds better than negotiating a contract. It is important that negotiators record what was agreed, or not agreed, during the negotiation and NOT after the event. If negotiators are unable to agree when they are sitting together face-to-face, they will not be able to do so later. If the discussions cannot reach agreement, it is necessary to carry on negotiating until both parties can.

ARBITRATORS are used when a tribunal or person adjudicates a disagreement between parties instead of going to legislation. Arbitrators exercise arbitrary power by making an award and the negotiators usually accept the decision. Negotiators unable to settle a dispute refer the matter to a mutually acceptable third party who receives submission from each side (oral or written) and then pronounces judgement. The UK Government's Advisory Conciliation and Arbitration Service (ACAS) provides an example.

Negotiating with people without AUTHORITY is not acceptable, since it leaves the parent organisation to seek concessions from the organisation in exchange for an agreement.

BARGAINING is obtaining something highly valued by one

party in exchange for something of less value to the other party. When a party is hungry he or she buys food for cash. Having bought food, they value the food more than the cash. The party selling the food values cash more than food or the seller would keep the food and manage without the cash. At the moment of exchange each party gets a bargain. This is so for all bargains in the open market. If a party is coerced into buying or selling, the extent of coercion measures the lack of bargaining.

BID STRATEGIES: There are two bidding strategies: one-offer-only and negotiate. A one-offer-only strategy is either a tender in a competitive situation and is your 'best price' or it is a pre-emptive take-it-or-leave-it bid in a non-competitive situation. A negotiation strategy is employed where direct contact with the client is possible. Your offer contains a realistic negotiation margin.

BLUFFING is almost always counter-productive. Bluffing means you live dangerously, which is exhilarating from the security of your arm chair, but it is risky in the real world of business.

BUYING SIGNALS: See them and stop your offers. Send one, and the offer stops. This is because buying signals show a willingness to settle on the terms of the current offer, so why offer more?

COD (Cash on Delivery): The purchaser pays cash upon delivery of the goods. No credit is allowed. The cash is collected by the deliverer of the goods, who deducts expenses and passes on the net amount to the supplier. Alternatively, the deliverer pays the net amount to the supplier before delivery, and collects the gross amount on delivery. Using COD is advisable if the purchaser is unknown to you, is a financial risk, is known as a late payer or it is necessary for your own CASH FLOW.

COERCION: When facing conflict of interest, you have two choices: attempt to coerce your opponent into CAPITULA-TION, or attempt to avoid capitulation by seeking an accommodation with him or her. Coercion involves THREATS, accommodation involves negotiation. Coercion can be a two-way process with each side attempting to win by coercing the other with threats. The negotiator risks having to implement his mutual threats and suffers the costs of the consequences: courts, strikes and wars are expensive. Your goal is to win, but you are constrained by the cost of implementing your threats. Negotiation aims to share the prize of agreement without paying too high a price for agreeing.

COLLATERAL: Something you need when borrowing somebody else's money. It can be a little of the property your company owns or a promise to pay from something you expect to own. Almost anything that the lender will accept as sufficient to cover for the risk of lending you money, is collateral. It can be something absolutely worthless when separated but valuable when together (the lender holds one part, the other party keeps the other). Borrowers arrange a loan against an item of equal or greater value than the loan. If you default on the loan, the lender gains possession of the pledged item and makes a profit by selling it at its true value, like the economics of pawnbroking.

COLLECTIVE BARGAINING: Jointly determined rules for the use of labour in employment. The rules are negotiated by agents of the employees (unions, staff associations) either directly with an employer or with an agent of the employer (an association of employers within a locality or in a line of business).

COMMISSION is payment for services rendered, for exceeding sales targets, for introducing clients. You should set your commission as a percentage of GROSS rather than NET value. The gross value of an income stream is larger than the net value. Therefore, you get more commission (conversely, if you are the person paying the commission).

COMMUNICATION: Message sent from one negotiator to another. If you do not communicate at all, you don't know what they want and they don't know what you want. Even if you are communicating, it is not certain that either of you will find out the other's needs. Messages are misunderstood, misinterpreted and mislaid. The message you sent may not be the one that is received. They may entirely miss the significance of the message you are communicating. They may not believe what you are saying, could doubt the provenance of the message and could be at a total loss to understand you because your message does not make sense.

CONCESSION DILEMMAS: The gap between the current offers of the two negotiators is created by a desire not to concede everything. If you are in conflict with the other negotiator as to the extent of your mutual concessions, you should aim to do better than CAPITULATION. Questions with uncertain answers include how much you must move, how far the other party will move, whether your proposals are acceptable or genuinely unacceptable!

CONCILIATION is an alternative form of dispute resolution. The aim is to reconcile the parties in dispute not to judge between them. Useful in fractious cases where the normal relationship between the parties has broken down and negotiations have deadlocked. Where inter-personal conflicts obscure a proper sense of balance the actual issues in dispute can be lost in a mutual bout of MARTYRDOM.

CONTINGENCY PRICING: Method of pricing an uncertain value. Forecasting is neither an art nor a science, it is an opinion. Valuations of the future worth of a business deal are as variable as the parties' interests. Buyers understate future worth, sellers exaggerate it. Then, to set the price for the business, the buyer offers a compromise valuation, which is less than the seller is wanting. In addition, the buyer offers a contingency price agreement. If the future conforms to the seller's opinion, the buyer pays an increasing schedule of prices. If the future conforms to the buyer's valuation, the seller receives nothing extra. Buyer's downside: the future is a result of the buyer's beneficial contribution, and not just the intrinsic worth of future business. The seller depends on the buyer's efforts and not on the value of the business when the seller owned it. Seller's downside: the buyer controls the business and can influence its future performance to understate its true worth. The buyer gains a business worth more than was paid, by treading water until the contingency agreement expires. Negotiable issues include:

- Is worth based on gross or net income?

- How long is the contingency agreement for?
- Is the seller's price set at last offer, or something less?
- Is the buyer's initial price set as last offer or something more?

CO-OPERATIVE STYLE: Negotiators are co-operative antagonists. Antagonisms arise from your conflicting or competing goals; your co-operation arises from the fact that DEADLOCK leaves you both worse off than COMPROMISE. You do not have malevolent designs, you are not distrustful, nor are you naively open. You understand why the other negotiator is hesitant about openness, but do not suspect his motives. If he SIGNALS, you respond but not recklessly; if he makes PROPOSALS, you search for bridges between his requirements and yours. You expect to TRADE for an AGREEMENT and you intend to honour that agreement. You also know how to switch into a COMPETITIVE STYLE if circumstances demonstrate it to be necessary.

DEADLINES can help or hinder depending upon who discloses that they have one. Deadlines put you under pressure. If you have to get the goods by Friday, your negotiating leverage crumbles on Thursday. If you must terminate the negotiation by New Year's Day, your biggest concessions appear on New Year's Eve. If you are up against a lead time for ordering materials for a major project, your buyer power diminishes, but this pressure is as nothing compared to the pressure you attract if you disclose your deadlines to the other negotiator. He or she will take advantage of your predicament. Whatever else the disclosure does, it must stiffen their resolve not to move in giant steps towards you; they know that you will soon be leaping towards them. Hence, don't disclose deadlines that the other negotiator has no other means of knowing about.

DELAYING TACTICS: Time changes the balance of power. Take two belligerent nations reconsidering the future of their war. When should they sue for peace? When there is a stalemate? But the fortunes of war often swing from side to side. One side's forces are pressing ahead to a devastating offensive; will the losing side be ameanable to negotiations for peace? Not if it believes it can stem the enemy's offensive and can redress the balance of power. What of the side whose armies are poised for final victory. Should it sue for peace and rob its forces of their triumph? Negotiations are unlikely while each side has different opinions of their fortunes.

EIGHT-STEP APPROACH: Method of anaylising negotiation as a process that goes through eight common steps, no matter what the negotiation is about, how big or small the stakes, who is conducting it, or where it is taking place. First developed between 1972—74 as a training aid for negotiating skills courses for industrial relations managers, it was applied to commercial negotiating skills training in 1975. It is widely used throughout the world in its original form and numerous versions ("Four phases; 'five-steps:', six-steps' etc) (After Gavin Kennedy, J Benson and J McMilland, Managing Negotiations, London, Hutchinson, 3rd ed 1987, 1980) (Ref 2). The eight steps are:

Prepare	Argue	Signal
Propose	Package	Bargain
Close	Agree	

Negotiators spend varying amounts of time in each step , they pass back and forth between the steps and they use different combinations, techniques, behaviours and tactics for each step. The anaylsis does not imply that negotiators rigidly make orderly progress through the steps, or that there is a prescriptive inference that they should do so. Based on observation of, and participation in, actual negotiations, the approach identifies the main activities of the process of negotiating a settlement, assesses the contribution of specific tactics and behaviours to the progress of the negotiations, and forms the core material of a negotiating skills training programme.

EQUITY: A much underused asset. Is the essence of raising your NET WORTH and to use other people's money to do so: your EQUITY is a useful instrument for LEVERAGE. You borrow multiples of your equity to purchase, or fund, wealth-creating investments. Equity is the difference between the value of an asset and what you borrow to acquire it. If you own the asset clear of all borrowing, then you have 100% of the equity at your disposal.

FAIT ACCOMPLI TACTIC: The deal is done and you defy them to undo it. Fait accompli tactics shift power to the doer and raise the stakes if counter sanctions are applied.

FINAL OFFER: If you make one, mean it, otherwise don't make one. Declaring an offer to be final' is risky. Turning a final offer into a 'final offer but one' (or two or three) is disastrous for credibility.

GREED: Many negotiators have created DEADLOCK from compromise by being too greedy. If you do not intend to be greedy, only ambitious, but the other negotiator perceives it as greed, then he or she will resent your behaviour. Resentment provokes resistance. Your price is just too high, and the project is dropped, leaving you with nothing; or they agree to pay, acquire your property and they don't pay up.

INCENTIVE is a carrot and stick approach to motivation. Offer an incentive for measurable performance and some people respond. Incentive gifts; are a thriving industry as an aid to motivating effort from a jaded sales force. The gifts include holidays, household extras, 'executive selections' (expensive toys), marketing aids, restaurant meals, weekend hotel breaks for two, car accessories and such like. Buyer's gifts cover a smaller range but have to be more discreet if given to buyer staff and not to the company.

INFORMATION can help or hinder negotiations. It can be valuable, as when you discover how badly they need your consent and co-operation. However, disclosing your needs can damage your stance.

LETTER OF CREDIT facilitates foreign trade. Terms are negotiable. If exporting, require the importer to open a credit with your bank for the value of the goods plus the agreed extras (CIF or FOB).

- Confirmed: importer's bank guarantees payment on production of appropraite shipping documents.
- Irrecoverable: to prevent importer refusing payment on any pretext.

- Transferable: to enable you to endorse it for other transactions.
- Divisible: to enable you to use it for part payment on other deals.

LINKING opens up bargaining possibilities. Presented with a list of demands, or an offer with more than one element, you must decide how to handle the total proposal. Do you deal with each issue seperately by treating each one as a distinct mini-negotiation, or do you link them together on the basis that nothing is agreed upon or everything is agreed upon?

MANDATE limits a negotiator's authority. Discretion is a heavy responsibility. If exceeded in the view of those to whom you are accountable, it can cause considerable problems, even to the point of repudiation of what you agreed. Employees often require their representatives not to accept any proposals from the company withour full reference back to them for approval. They also mandate their representatives to demand a particular item and to accept nothing less than the mandated demand. This ties the hands of the employee negotiators. It may be a tactic to enhance commitment; it may be an absolutely immovable stance taken because feelings are high, or because determination is complete.

How can you handle a mandate demand? Not by conceding it merely because the representatives have imposed a mandate, not unless you want to be on the receiving end of lots of other mandate demands. Is the mandate a commitment tactic. Is the mandate solid evidence of the true feelings of the employees? If it is, treat it like any other expression of feeling; firmly, though gently, but with regard to your INTEREST.

MOTIVATION: Other people have baser motives than ourselves. This harmless delusion becomes dangerous when we act as if other negotiators respond only to the motivations we ascribe to them.

Ascribed Motive	Competitive Action	Co-operation Action
Fear	Threaten	Assure
Pride	Mock	Flatter
Hatred	Hate	Love

Ascribed Motive	Competitive Action	Co-operation Action
Loyality	Exploit	Reward
Money	Minimise	Maximise
Love	Withhold	Requite
Desire	Frustrate	Satisfy
Jealousy	Excite	Calm
Ambition	Block	Assist

If the other negotiators are not motivated by your ascriptions, your actions make no sense to them unless they ascribe to you the motivation suggested by your behaviour.

NEGOTIATION SKILLS: What distinguishes the above-average negotiator from the rest? Views vary. Some go as far as to believe that negotiators are born, not made. Versions of the 'born' school ascribe the qualities of good negotiators some-times to race, which is limiting for the rest of humankind who negotiate too. Sometimes to gender, which is even more ludicrous, and sometimes to the mysticism of genitics. These explanations are non-starters. While not everybody competes in decathlons, or writes music etc everybody negotiates, and if some are born to it, this still leaves the rest of us doing the best we can. Given that the 'born' principle can never be tested (because by definition, anybody who is any good is born to it and the rest are not), we are left with trying to establish exactly what above average negotiators do that is different from poorer negtiators.

NOT NEGOTIABLE is a pressure tactic. Set out a non-negotiable area and refuse to budge and force the other negotiator to accept your exclusion tactic. The problem comes if what you are excluding from the negotiaton is the central issue that the other negotiator wishes to negotiate about. Some issues are non-negotiable, and the negotiator would prefer to resolve the dispute by other means sooner than permit a negotiation on a shared issue. Merely excluding issues does not make them non-negotiable, otherwise negotiators the world over would narrow the negotiable issues to the ones they felt strongest about, or the ones they were least concerned about.

ORDER TAKER: a sign of a jaded salesforce. Sellers who merely meet customers to take their regular orders are missing opportunities to negotiate better orders. It is also cheaper for a company selling them from a regular low value list to use a telephone sales operation. Not only are all outlets covered this way, but with on-line direct input into a computer system, merely calling a supplier to give an order as a sign of a jaded buying operation. What special offers are available? You won't know if you don't ask, unless they volunteer to tell you.

PERSONAL RELATIONSHIPS: never underestimate their value. Only trespass on them once. Do not rely on them. While you seek to cultivate sound personal relationships based on demonstrated trust and reliability, you must recognise that other people's commitment to your interest is fragile. Commercial negotiators, diplomats and bargaining agents inevitably form relationships, if only from getting to know each other. These relationships are important however tentative they may be, for negotiating with somebody you do not know is more difficult than negotiating with somebody you do know (ask sellers whether they prefer cold calling to hot leads). The basic principle of establishing a personal negotiating relationship is not to push the other negotiator into the ground by CO-ERCION; it is not even to push them to your TARGET PRICE; it is to assist them to achieve their OBJECTIVES within the boundaries of your own. In short, don't take undue advantage of their predicament.

PREPARATION: Jewel in the crown of negotiation. Get this right and your performance in the negotiation dramatically improves. The best preparation is knowing your business better than any one else. If you don't know your business well enough, you can rely on your rivals to teach you.

PRIORITIES are best sorted out in PREPARATION, not while negotiating face-to-face. Objectives in negotiation are not all weighted with the same degree of priority otherwise their would be room for movement. Some issues are more important than others and their ranking should be decided beforehand. The most important issues are "MUST GETS" — you genuinely prefer no agreement at all to not securing your "must gets".

Other issues can be graded into "should gets" and "would likes". These are issues that you can TRADE to get agreement.

Events in the negotiation could prompt you to revise your priorities and you might wish to ADJOURN to consider the changing circumstances. Establishing your priorities is meant to be an organising not stultifying activity. The act of prioritising objectives or issues ensures a firm grasp of the detail of the negotiated issues rather than opening with a hazy notion of what is important to you.

PSYCHOLOGY: The psychology of negotiating is a complex subject. People are different. Smart people believe they know what is going on and the rest of us are left wondering. The two great drives of human endeavour are our motivations and whatever we perceive the world outside to be. These do not always match. Taking motivations, these are best summed up by Maslow's hierarchy of needs (after A H Maslow, A Theory of Human Motivation, Psychological Review, 50 (1943) pp 370—96 and Motivation and Personality, New York, Harper and Row, 1954). Human needs are expressed in a ascending order of importance as each level of need is satisfied.

RAPPORT: Helpful, but not sufficient to secure a negotiated agreement. It is helpful because the relationship is positive between the negotiators. Lack of rapport certainly can inhibit agreement, or slow down progress towards it. It is helpful to establish rapport by matching your pace to the other negotiators (particularly when negotiating across a cultural divide), by taking a genuine interest in his contribution to the discussion by asking questions that indicate your interest and by steering gently rather than agressively towards the settlement you are looking for.

SPLIT THE DIFFERENCE: Settlement tactic. Negotiators stuck on two numbers can move to a settlement "splitting the difference". You offer 80, they offer 40, splitting the difference gives you 60. It sounds fair and equitable and sometimes it is. Other times, it is not. It can also be expensive; perhaps you can not afford to split the difference.

STRESS: Negotiations is a stressfull activity. You are anxious about the outcome, emotional about the behaviour, unsure of the implication of offers, worried about their intentions, concerned about not doing as well as you or your peers expect and generally tense as well as tired. Stress cannot be eliminated; it can be reduced. The professional negotiator tries not to take things personally, tries to separate the issues from the personalities and tries to concentrate on interests rather than issues. Basically you should slow down the pace (ask more QUESTIONS), relax before and after sessions, and set REALISTIC rather than fanciful targets.

SWITCH SELLING: Seller's ADD-ON tactic. You think you are negotiating to buy a deluxe car, but before you know what is happening one finds oneself in discussion about acquiring the super deluxe car. The seller has "switch sold" the buyer up the range.

TARGET PRICE: The negotiating objective you wish to reach if you can. It is your desired, best terms, objective, what you would like to settle on. Whether you are open with your target price, or another price somewhere slightly above or below it (your SHAM OFFER) depends on how you perceive your prospects. If you open at your target you are likely to be forced to move away from it by the other negotiator (unless they surrender to your first offer).

TRADEABLE: The currency of the bargaining process. Movement is secured by offering to TRADE something that you have for something that they have. Anything that you can trade is tradeable.

WHAT IF?: Questioning techniques to elucidate potential negotiating issues. Useful techniques when faced with DEAD-LOCK. It helps explore possible avenues down which solutions to the deadlock may be found. For example, "what if we were to consider delaying the payment deadlines, would that help you with your budgeting?" Or, "what if we merged our two companies into a joint venture, would that meet your concerns about disclosing proprietary information?"

Also useful when faced with a proposition in a field you are not familiar with. The offer may look alright but you have no criteria against which to judge it. Ask "what if?" questions about everything imaginable in the proposition and note what information comes out of the answers.

CHAPTER 11

THE SINGLE EUROPEAN MARKET

Introduction

The creation of a single market within Europe was inevitable with the formation of the European Community. By the end of 1992, the trade barriers which prevent Europe being a single market will have come down and many changes have already been agreed.

The changes occuring could affect a business at any time, so, all firms need to prepare NOW to meet the challenge and seize the opportunities afforded to them. During the next few years many businesses could double their present size — or halve it. A summary of the important stages is given below. An appendix to this chapter summarises the literature and help available from the government (and other agencies) to help UK businesses prepare for, and venture into, exporting their offerings to the Single European Market.

Single European Market (SEM)

The major aim of the European Community (EC) is the creation of the SEM by December 1992. This was originally stated as a prime objective of the Treaty of Rome and was intended to create a single European trading block which would match the USA and USSR in terms of output, production and population. A first stage in the process was to be the removal of trade tariffs. Here, internal tariffs on industrial goods had been largely eliminated by 1977 but numerous obstacles to trade within the Community still remained. The objectives of an SEM by 1992 (originally proposed by Jacques Delors, President of the European Commission,) were formalised in the Commission's White Paper 'Completing the Internal Market' published in June 1985.

The Barriers to Trade

The barriers to trade, and benefits from liberalisation, were identified, and quantified by, Paolo Cecchini in "The European Challenge 1992 — the benefits of a Single Market" which was published on behalf of the European Commission. The problem was that, although internal tariffs had largely been eliminated by 1977, substantial trade obstacles were still in existence. The barriers to trade were identified as:

- Physical barriers — in particular frontier delays and administrative burdens imposed on goods in transit;
- Technical barriers — inter country differences in technical regulations, standards and differences in business law;
- Fiscal barriers — in particular differing vat and excise duties.

The 1985 White Paper also identified the following further barriers:

- Restriction on competition for public sector contracts — which, in practice, favoured domestic supplies;
- Special arrangements for specific industries, eg the Multifibre Arrangement adopted by individual countries and;
- The agricultural sector — as a consequence of the Common Agricultural Policy.

The White Paper's Liberalisation Programme has three main components:

- The removal of physical barriers to the movement of goods and people.
- The removal of technical barriers covering quality, standards, public procurement and regulation.
- The removal of fiscal barriers, eg the harmonisation of VAT rates.

The Cecchini Report

This report by Paolo Cecchini mentioned earlier , estimated that the liberalisation measures would result in econonmic gains to the SEM of the following order:
TABLE 1

Static Welfare Gains:	70bm—190bm ECU's (2½ — 6½% of the EC 1988 GDP)
Increased Growth Rate:	1% pa
Increased Employment:	2 million additional jobs
Reduced consumer prices (% GDP)	6%
External Balance	1%
Budgetary Balance (% GDP)	1%

The SEM can therefore be seen to be a source of major benefit to governments, business and consumers.

The DTI has made available information packs to tell businesses what changes are taking place and these include check-lists that will help any business to prepare to take action now (1).

There is an abundance of information and statistics available to guide firms and, as an appendix to this chapter, many relevant papers and offers of help are listed. In March 1989 the Commission of European Communities published "A Community of Twelve: Key Figures" which gives in pictorial form many statistics that firms may find useful. Data on population, trade between member states, GDP consumption (as a % of total household consumption) are given later in this chapter.

Benefits of the SEM

There are many benefits which will become available to those businesses that are well prepared and in a position to take advantage of them. Some of the main advantages open to business are as follows:

- The dismantling of all barriers will open up new opportunities for British business. With the accession of Spain and Portugal to the EC in 1986 there is a domestic market of 323 million people — nearly as many as the United States and Japan combined. (See Table 2 and Figure 1).
- Completing a Single European Market will reduce business costs, stimulate increased efficiency and encourage the creation of wealth and jobs.
- The EC is the United Kingdom's largest export market and its importance is increasing.
- In 1972 the 11 other countries which are now SEM member states took 33% of UK exports; ten years later this figure was 44% and is now 50% in all. UK exports of goods to the community totalled £41 billion in 1988.

Other member states now account for 52% of UK imports compared with 36% in 1972. However, there is still room for considerable growth in every EC market.

- The Single European Act (SEA) commits the EC to the aim of progressively establishing a single market over a period expiring on 31 December 1992. The single market is defined as "an area without internal frontiers in which the free movement of goods, persons, services and capital is insured in accordance with the provision of the Treaty".

Figure 1

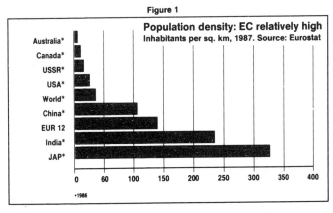

Population density: EC relatively high
Inhabitants per sq. km, 1987. Source: Eurostat

Australia*
Canada*
USSR*
USA*
World*
China*
EUR 12
India*
JAP*

0   60   100   150   200   250   300   350   400

*1986

Fig 1 shows the relatively high population density of the SEM alongside that of other countries in the world.

- The SEA also incorporates a series of important Treaty reforms to speed up the decision making by extending majority voting to virtually all the major areas of the Single Market Programme. In the past, progress was often held up in the unanimous voting requirements which applied before the SEA came into force.

Table 2 shows the populations of the countries in the SEM (including the UK) illustrating the increased size of the new market.

TABLE 2 (Source: Readers Digest Associations, Atlas of the World 1987)
Population of EC Countries

Country	Population (millions) 1987
Denmark	9.9
W. Germany	1.2
France	55.6
Greece	9.9
Eire (S. Ireland)	3.5
Italy	57.3
Luxembourg	0.4
Netherlands	14.7
Portugal	10.3
Spain	38.8
UK	56.9
	318.4

Figure 2 illustrates Gross Domestic Product per head in community countries.

Finally, Figure 3 shows a comparison of distribution of expenditure as a % of total household consumption on accommodation, leisure, miscellaneous, food, transport and clothing items for 1986.

Any firm considering venturing into the SEM, or any other potential overseas market, may find the following checklist helpful in formulating its marketing strategy in order to ensure that it maximises its potential for success. This checklist is not exhaustive and may need to be amended to meet the needs of

Gross domestic product: a relatively rich Community . . .

GDP per head* (world = 100, 1986)

Figure 2. Source: Eurostat

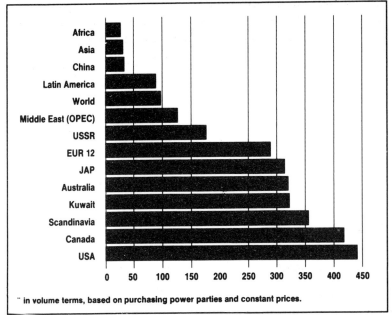

* in volume terms, based on purchasing power parties and constant prices.

any particular organisation. It should, however, provide a useful basis on which to proceed.

Action Strategy

Key questions should be:

- Has the Market changed our offering(s)?
- Should the firm look upon the EC as its prime market rather than just the UK?
- How will the firm become vulnerable to more competition in present markets?
- Is the firm's management structure appropriate to exploit new opportunities or defend its position?
- Should the firm form links, merge or acquire a business in order to broaden its range of products to strengthen the enterprise? (This is discussed later in the Chapter)

Figure 3

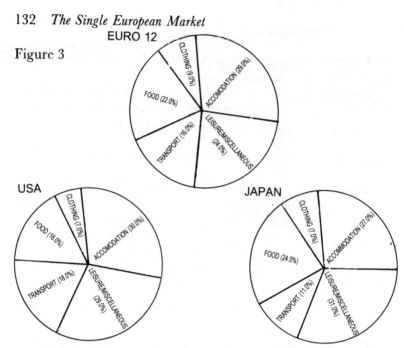

EURO 12

USA

JAPAN

• What training in language skills are needed to be ready for the Single Market?

In terms of marketing, it becomes necessary to work to an appropriate checklist such as:

• Identify those countries the firm is not selling to, where sales are limited and why.
• Which markets become more accessible and when?
• What new customers can we reach and how?
• What are the firm's competitors and what is known about their marketing strengths, weaknesses, products and prices?
• How do competitors sell and what is the structure of distribution in the market? (refer back to the DTI "country profiles" for help in this area).
• Market information. Has the firm proper information and statistics? Where can the firm find this? Get it immediately (Ref 2 will help initially).
• Has the firm:
    —made or does it plan to make exploratory visits?
    —attended trade shows and exhibitions?

- Has the business commissioned any market research or visited the statistics office?
- Has it got information on Government help in obtaining low cost market research or contacted the European Chamber of Commerce on this subject?

How suitable are the firm's products/services?

- Obtain basic data by contacting the BSI to ask if there is an industrial standard for the firm's product, set by national authorities or by a leading supplier.
- Find out if, and how, the offering would need to be adapted to the needs of industrial or commercial users.
- Does the quality of the offering match the needs of the market?
- Is the products packaging suitable? Can the firm compete on product quality and price?
- Does the firm have details of the new competition to its existing markets and has it identified potential competitors and assessed their competitive strengths in terms of price and quality.
- What are the buying plans of the firm's existing customers.

Is the business organised to learn about the wider market and carry out promotion effectively?

- Who will be responsible for marketing to the SEM?
- Who will collect and assess marketing information?
- Is the firm getting help and advice from the DTI's Marketing and Export Initiatives?

In the sales and distribution areas checklists would set down and answer the following questions:
How do you reach customers?

- Has the firm investigated the trade structure, such as wholesaler and retailers and identified buying points?
- Has the firm examined different selling approaches, including brokers and agents?

- How do competitors use advertising, promotion and trade discounts?
- Has the firm considered regional test marketing, established its sales targets and decided on a sales and promotion budget?
- Has the firm decided on its selling organisation, what sales literature is needed, and, has it considered the need for redesign for new customers and arranged translations where necessary.
- Has the marketing function decided how to advertise?
- Have differences in national media available and cost been assessed? Has the budget been decided?
- How will the firm provide an after-sales service?
- Have the relative merits and costs of direct provision or subcontracting been considered?

In preparing a distribution checklist a firm should note the importance of getting to the customer on time. More customers and destinations pose distribution challenges (once again the DTI country profiles will help here). New transport routes and new services will require study.

What changes are needed in the firm's distribution needs?

Has the firm?

- Identified new locations to be served and estimated the increased volume of products?
- Found out about the structure of distribution in new markets, and considered speed of delivery and size of loads?
- Decided between direct delivery and the need for warehousing as well as,
- Decided on warehouse locations, defined adequate stock levels and how to maintain them.?

What organisation does the firm need to support its distribution?

- Has the firm decided on information handling requirements and how to control remote locations.

For enterprise supplies services it is necessary to decide:

- How it will reach new customers.
- Will you be able to provide a service directly from the U.K. or is a presence in local markets required.
- Has it considered the relative advantages and costs of: establishing a subsidiary or branch?
- linking with local firms?
- using an agent or brokers?

Checklists for the areas of production, finance, purchasing and product development are suggested by the DTI in its Action Checklist for Business published in September 1988 by the DTI Central Offices of Information (1). Further practical help is available through the DTI's Enterprise Initiative that has been discussed previously. Useful telephone numbers are given below. The Statistics and Market Intelligence Library (SMIL) and Product Data Store is a publicly accessible library of overseas market intelligence that can be contacted on 071–215 5444.

The Exports Europe branch covers all 12 communities and can be contacted by telephoning 071–215 5549 (Multi-country enquiries).

Export Intelligence service details can be obtained from the local DTI office.

Centres for European Business Information can be contacted in London, Department of Employment, Small Firms Services (telephone 071–730 8115), The Birmingham Chamber of Industry and Commerce (telephone 021–454 6171), at Newcastle, Northern Development (telephone 091–261 5131) and also at Glasgow Strathclyde Euroinfocentre (telephone 041–221 0999).

Contents of progress on EC legislation can be obtained on the DTI's Hotline (081–200 1992).

The Exporting Company and the SEM

In chapter 1 of his text 'Export for the Small Business' (3) Deschampsneufs comments that "There probably never has been a better time to become involved with export, for two main reasons. First there is a noticeable change taking place in international trade. For many years we have lived in a world of mass production . . . the aim of the producers has been to provide the greatest quantity of goods at the lowest possible price for the greatest number of consumers. Growth has been the aim of almost all companies, on the basis that the larger the company, the more efficient it becomes, and the greater its profits. As a result the consumer is offered increasingly standard products . . . yet today there are signs of revolt by consumers against standard products . . . .

Secondly, there is a corresponding increase in the demand for a greater variety of life styles . . . we can see the growth of the 'Do it yourself market' for instance . . . people make their own wine, bake their own bread and service their own cars."

The significance of this development is that more and more specialised products are being demanded. This is where the small business has its greater strength . . . it is they who are in the best position to supply specialised products and personalised services. The SEM, when it begins in 1992, will present many opportunities for British companies since it will be dealing with a greater population with more diverse patterns of behaviour.

Regarding the legislative impact of 1992 on small businesses, and the Small Business Research Trust 1992 Survey, the National Westminster Bank has published a Small Business Digest (1992 special edition) freely available through any high street branch.

This very useful, easy to read, 20 page booklet deals with:

a) **The Legislative Impact of 1992 on Small Businesses**
   1. The importance of small business on the European stage.
   2. The institutions of the European Community.
   3. Community legislation.
   4. Treaty of Rome.

b) **Protectionism and the free movement of goods and services**
   1. Discriminatory Taxation.
   2. Custom duties and equivalent charges.

3. Public procurement contracts.
4. Consumer protection.
5. Harmonisation of standards.
6. Financial services.
7. Indirect taxation — VAT and excise duties.
8. State aid.

c) **The legal implications of 1992 for small business**
1. EC competition rules.

Get Started Now

Before discussing the smaller firm, some comments, made by Lord Young, Margaret Thatcher and John Major may offer some help to smaller companies.

In the DTI's Single Market Publication of October 1988 the main article entitled 'Now for Action', quotes Lord Young as making comments that will help to reinforce this chapter. In terms of awareness of the SEM there has been progress since the DTI formally launched the 'Open for Business Campaign'. However, at this time too few firms had begun to prepare seriously enough for action. Lord Young outlined how the DTI and associated agencies can help firms to prepare to get started now.

In this article, Lord Young made the following comments:—

"1992 is certainly on everyone's lips now; indeed you can hardly open a newspaper or switch on television without seeing something about the magic date. Many firms are featuring 1992 in their own advertising."

"Just 12 months ago very few people in business in this country — even senior people in large companies — knew much about the Single Market — under one in six know of the 1992 target date for completing the Single Market — a staggering figure for a country which does half of all its trade with the European community."

"When we formally launched the Open for Business Campaign" I set a target of 90 per cent awareness of the Single Market by the end of this year."

"The battle for awareness has already been won but awareness is only the first step".

"The all too easy '1992' label brings its own problems especially if it encourages firms to believe that they still have three or four years to prepare. 1992 is no magic date when everything will happen. 31 December 1992 is the date when a long and complex legislative process will be completed."

"The changes for the Single Market are already happening. Decisions are being taken month by month."

"I want British Business to be the best prepared in the Community. That means two big challenges:

- Awareness counts for little unless business readily gets to grips with the implications of the fundamental changes taking place in the Community's trading rules. There is no substitute for doing your homework. The DTI has prepared the most comprehensive service anywhere in the Community. Use it.
- What matters at the end of the day, is not awareness or even understanding, but action by every firm in the country.

Our survey showed that fewer than one firm in three has begun to prepare seriously for action. That represents a substantial increase since I announced our campaign. But that is a long way short of being satisfactory. I want to see the figure grow rapidly during the next 12 months. Everyone will need to consider an action strategy and take decisions to respond to the Single Market Challenge.

DTI's Action Checklists outline the issues and gives sources of further information and advice.

DTI's Enterprise Initiative provides one of the key ways of preparing for the Single Market launched at the start of the year, it is already helping many businesses help themselves to achieve a more competitive edge. No one now has the excuse for missing out. The Single Market is our opportunity. Go out and seize it."

In the same publication appears a list of Single Market events, that is, details of conferences and seminars being organised in every part of the country by Chambers of Commerce, trade associations and other organisations. Further information can be obtained by telephoning 071–215 4770.

Smaller Firms

In the above publication there is a useful article discussing small firms and the Single Market with sections covering the following:

- Preparing Now
- Opportunities
- Competition
- How to find out more

In the context of urging the smaller firm to join in the EC by offering its service or product, much literature has been written aimed mainly at giving motivation and guidance. These are found in earlier references within this text. The CBI has urged export aid (4) for the smaller business who could increase exports, and make a vital contribution towards reducing Britain's trade deficit. It is suggested that more should be done to meet their requirement, particularly by the British Overseas Trade Board. This emerges from a CBI survey of nearly 200 small businesses. The need for action was underlined by the chairman of the CBI's smaller firms council when he announced the survey results. A particular problem area appeared to be in securing access to good market intelligence and establishing sales and distribution returns and a special problem reported for firms offering professional services was the lack of market information. This was a significant finding revealed by the survey when plans to have mutual recognition of professional qualificationsin the Single European Market are taken into consideration. The survey showed that there was 'much potential' for small firms to increase their European share. The most scope for increasing export activity lay with middle-sized businesses, with between 21 and 50 employees.

The guide entitled '1992 Guide For The Smaller Businesses' available from Price Waterhouse, the chartered accountants (5), reports that "The sad truth is that there are indeed hundreds of millions of pounds worth of grants, low interest loans and other funds, but very little in the hands of business entrepreneurs and smaller firms. Most of the money is with the Government's Enterprise Initiative Scheme and a great deal of it is not being claimed".

Price Waterhouse's independent services director comments that: "Business cannot afford to be complacent about the Single European Market". This is true not only for multi nationals, but also the smaller independent businesses and adds: "Those who believe 1992 will have little or no impact on them are in for a rude awakening".

Small businesses are advised to contact the trade department's hotline and the EC's British centres for more information. Most of these services are free.

The above guide also suggests that there is a direct link between export performance and someone in a company being able to speak in a customer's language. The skills are taught at Language-Export Centres. Further valuable help is available from the DTI's "1992 — for you", an action guide for the smaller business (6) which deals not only with markets, products and services, how the Single Market affects the smaller firm and finance but lists useful sources of further help for the smaller firm through local advice "clubs". trade associations, public sector contracts, finding business partners, documentation and payment as well as other booklets about 1992.

Much information is now being offered by many agencies and chapter 13 gives a summary of help being offered by:
The British Overseas Trade Board BOTD;
The Department of Enterprise DTI;
The Council of Chambers of Commerce in Central Europe CBCC;
The Confederation of British Industry;
Most Major banks and;
Many Accounting firms.
This chapter will hopefully help business readers to identify

those areas which will be of maximum use to them and prevent their obtaining and reading through a vast amount of literature to locate a particular topic vital to their firm.

REFERENCES AND FURTHER READINGS

References

1. An Action Checklist for Business, DTI and Central Office of Information, HMSO, September 1988.
2. A Community of Twelve: Key Figure, Commission of European Communities, March 1989, available from 8 Storeys Gate, London SW13 3AT, telephone 071–222 8122; 4 Cathedral Row, Cardiff CF1 O8G telephone Cardiff 371 631; 7 Alva Street, Edinburgh EH2 4PH, telephone Edinburgh 225 2058.
3. Dechampsneufs H: Export for the Small Business, 2nd Ed. Kogan Page.
4. CBI, Centrepoint 108 New Oxford Street, London WC1A 1DV.
5. Price Waterhouse, 1992 Guide for Small Business, The Time, November 14 1989. Further details Enterprise Agencies and European Information Centres (dial operator for Freephone Enterprise) BOTB 071–215 7577, DTI 1992 hotline 081–200 1992.
6. Sunday Times 23 April 1989, Getting All the Facts For 1992.
7. The Times, 6 December 1989, Export Boost Essential for Growth.

Further Suggested Readings and Source for Growth

1. Fortune International, 28 August 1989, Main J. How To Go Global — And Why.
2. Fortune International, Special Issue No 26 Autumn 1989:
   a) The Challenge of Asia in the 1990's
   b) Understanding How Japan Works
   c) Doing Business in China Now

     d) The Tiger Behind Korea's Prowess
     e) Asia's Rising Export Powers
3. Fortune No.24 November 6 1989:
     a) America's Place in World Competition
     b) Japan's Big Knack for Coming Back
     c) Fortune Forecast on US Economy
4. Fortune Special Issue 29. Autumn 1989:
     a) The Smart Way to Go Global
     b) Promising Industries for 1990
5. Fortune No.20 September 15 1989:
     a) Where will Japan Strike Next?
     b) How Harley Beat Back The Japanese. A successful turnaround for a firm where quality was awful, manufacturing a mess. The managers bought the company and pulled off a celebrated turnaround.
6. Fortune No 18, 28 August 1989:
     a) Dudley J N. Strategies for the Single Market
     b) Who Runs Japan?
7. Fortune No.28, 18 December 1989, Kirkland Jn R1, Who gains for the new Europe? The author's answer to the question is "Almost everyone does and there's opportunity aplenty for deals. The combined GNP for East Germany, Hungary and Czechoslovakia is bigger than China's".
8. 'Which' February 1990 — The first of a new series on 1992, explaining to the general public and business what the SEM will mean to them in terms of the legislative impact etc. etc.

CHAPTER 12

INTERNATIONAL DIRECT MARKETING

Introduction

International Direct Marketing (IDM) allows the ambitious, market orientated organisation to extend its market overseas by:—

- Permitting the firm to communicate directly with a targeted market and personalising correspondence in the customer's own language;
- Allowing a selective approach to the chosen target population by testing the market through the use of a pre-paid response system before embarking upon a major marketing drive;
- Providing a cost effective approach towards marketing the firm's products as well as establishing a niche in the new, large market without high initial expense or investment;
- Allowing the marketing organisation to use a variety of promotional methods that are appropriate to each environment and adaptable to the legal requirements of each country;
- Offering a comprehensive world marketing mechanism and sophisticated postal system across the world, thus ensuring that the marketing reaches its intended target and;
- Having the support of a sophisticated, and proven, direct marketing industry both in the U.K and internationally.

IDM is the most comprehensive and cost-effective way of finding and developing international business and all firms, however large or small, that wish to enlarge their market are strongly advised to take steps to study IDM and make use of the many sources of help available to them because, in 1992, and after the international direct mail services of the various European postal organisations will play an extremely important role as a marketing tool that can reach those individual consumer groups that are beyond the reach of the mass market media techniques.

Customer feedback is an essential element in an organisation's market research. It is by understanding the geographic and demographic characteristics of these new markets that sellers can ensure a successful outcome. IDM can:—

- Provide accurate information about an organisations effectiveness when linked to a business reply service;
- Generate significant sales leads and direct sales by mail order;
- Use promotional techniques to elicit more than just a sales enquiry but build an invaluable database giving detailed customer profiles;
- Provide prospects with an easy, low cost route to the marketing company's offerings;
- Assist in market research and;
- Provide data for on-going analysis of geographic and demographic campaign successes both across Europe and internationally.

An important factor in international direct mail is the provision of a direct and economical response system through the International Business Reply Service (IBRS). For a small fee, the IBRS can help to make all of the selling firm's efforts more successful. A pre-paid response is the best way to ensure getting a reply. IBRS also measures the result of a direct marketing campaign as well as effectively increasing the number of respondants to mailshots. IBRS can thus:—

- Stimulate increased responses by making it easier for customers to reply at no expense to themselves;

- Return all replies direct to the designated U.K address, removing the need for additional handling and delay;
- Return all replies to the selling company by Airmail;
- Assist in building upon a mailing list of interest to overseas clients;
- Provide one design for all countries, thus reducing production costs and;
- Provide up to 1000 responses for a simple one-off fee to cover the licence and making no further charges for the first year.

Services Postaux Européens (SPE) was set up six years ago as the official society of postal organisations in Europe, with the aim of promoting direct marketing on both a national and international level.

The current membership of SPE encompasses both EC and non-EC countries and the 13 member countries are: Belgium, Denmark, Finland, France, Ireland, Luxembourg, Netherlands, Norway, Portugal, Sweden, Switzerland, Federal Republic of Germany and the UK.

Doing business in Europe generally means treating each country as a separate entity. Old traditions and outlooks cannot be changed overnight. Consultation can tone down these differences however. A pan-European approach can be helpful, particularly in the area of postal innovation and postal product development. The national post offices that are members of SPE evolved individually and are products of their own cultures both business-wise and nationally.

SPE provides a vehicle through which postal authorities of various backgrounds can exchange information and map out common strategies with the ultimate aim of providing homogenous postal products for the benefit of direct marketers. Operating in the complete European market is a demanding task and there are many hurdles that do not exist in other economic groupings, which must be overcome.

Overcoming National Hurdles

Variations in language, history, legislation and culture present challenges to those direct marketers that are working internationally. With the establishment of the Single European Market, however, life promises to be more simple, the removal of customs barriers being a first step in the right direction. Basic cultural differences will however persist.

The harmonisation process within the European Community is a formidable task that has absorbed vast amounts of energy and resources. A great deal has been accomplished and legislation is being harmonised in many areas, making it easier for both the private consumer and businesses to feel more at home outside their national borders.

One of the primary business needs today is for international services in every area, be it distribution, marketing or communications. The postal organisations of SPE recognise this need and are actively working together to create truly international postal products and services that can compete with the best currently available on the market, and a new agency has been set up to co-ordinate these efforts. The SPE also serves as an information pool in making the direct mail market clearer for direct marketers by providing up-to-date statistics on both the market itself and how it is developing.

In the six years since its formation SPE has made considerable progress. Starting as little more than a loose federation for providing better postal services and products for direct marketers SPE has become a closely knit organisation with well defined objectives, exchanging information between members with a view to harmonising postal services throughout Europe.

Internationalisation

In keeping with the process already underway among the postal services aimed at creating postal products that can compete on an equal basis with the best that the market can offer, a new agency has been set up.

The task of this agency, known as the International Post

Corporation (IPC), is to construct a framework of co-operation between several European postal administrations, define the conditions of international postal products, and see that agreed objectives are met. The IPC will thus be concerned with engineering the conditions under which international postal products can gain in importance in terms of improved reliability, greater flexibility and consistency, thus giving more body to the concept of product harmonization. Contractual responsibility is also a concept that will be built into postal products.

Understanding Direct Mail

Through surveys and statistical research SPE compiles regular reports on the various aspects of the direct marketing industry in order to measure how direct mail and direct marketing techniques are used from country to country, who is using them and why.

Direct Mail is a modern, developing industry that gains strength each year as it becomes even more sophisticated. However, learning to work successfully with any medium takes time and direct mail is no exception. Of course taking advantage of the experience of other users can be helpful.

Part of SPE's task, therefore, is to promote a greater understanding of direct mail and direct marketing techniques both to regular as well as to first time users and to encourage optimum use of these techniques.

Internationalising the Postal Services

The past years have witnessed dramatic changes in the way organisations do business, both in Europe and the World. Put simply, the globalisation of trade and communications has made it necessary for companies to operate on a transnational scale. Both the organisation and its environment have been revolutionised by new technologies. Communications are global, network systems have become standardised, software is now better and hardware cheaper. Telefax and electronic mail have opened new channels of direct communication. For marketing firms, marketing has had to recognise a switch away from a mass market approach. Segmentation, using direct mail and database marketing, for example, have become much more important than before.

Generally speaking, streamlined, more efficient business has played an important part in stimulating economic growth. Because the costs of doing business have been reduced, prices to consumers have been lowered in real terms. At the same time, other barriers are being removed. The growth of international courier services reflects business's greater need for speed in foreign markets that have been opened by the removal of trade barriers. Export business has grown markedly all round. The signs augur well for the future.

The European Consumer

Just as the business environment is undergoing radical change, consumer preferences are also changing radically due to increased affluence. Demographically, Europe is becoming a middle aged society — the proportion of teenagers in the population is slowly decreasing and there are more and more people in the 30—50 years age bracket. Present day developments indicate that more people will be self employed. With the increasing application of automation, up to a third of the working population could be working from home by the year 2000 if the same pattern is seen as in the US.

With more people self employed or retired there will be a greater demand for personal financial services. As the length of the average working week declines, people will spend more time in their homes and so will require home durables to replace services traditionally provided outside the home. Consumers will also expect products to be available when and where they want and at prices they can afford. With the focus increasingly on the home, shopping from and delivery to the home will grow in popularity.

In the international marketplace meanwhile, global brands will compete on a global scale. On the domestic market, in the meantime, traditional mass markets will have been replaced by specific, individual markets reflecting greater consumer affluence and changed consumer lifestyles.

New Competition and 1992

What is left of the postal monopolies is disintegrating as deregulation will make further inroads. Postal monopolies will only exist in future where they can be shown to be more efficient and more cost effective than alternative arrangements. Postal services will thus have to be co-ordinated internationally and be comprehensive enough to facilitate business-to-business and business-to-consumer communications and distribution. As business speeds up, many time sensitive documents and letters will be sent by fax and other electronic services. One important first step in this direction was the establishment of the CEPT agency, now called International Post Corporation (IPC).

New International Services

To provide international customers with better and more competitive services, the post offices plan new services incorporating concepts such as worldwide proof of delivery, worldwide tracking and tracing, optimum customs clearance and an extensive same-day service.

The products that will emerge from these concepts will build on existing strengths in the processing and distribution of time-sensitive letters and parcels to meet customers' needs for speed, reliability and convenience at competitive prices. These quality services will be backed by comprehensive marketing campaigns to international business with the underlying message that the post offices are fully committed to providing the high quality international services that business urgently needs.

For direct marketers, an international electronic mail service is being developed to send mail shots to customers in another country faster and more efficiently. Businesses in this scheme will be able to send their customer data and customer addresses down the line to a post office printer in the country of destination. There it will be printed and delivered to the customers locally.

The potential for other new services on a joint venture basis is also being looked at. Such new services could be in areas such as transport and distribution, marketing sales or media communications.

Postal Monopoly

The introduction of many such new services will mean upheavals in the internal organisations of the post offices. A minimum postal monopoly however seems necessary to guarantee an efficient, cost-effective service for businesses and households. Without such a minimum monopoly, it would be impossible for the post offices to provide direct marketers with an acceptable level of access to consumers.

The monopoly position of the post offices will no doubt be further eroded, especially at international level. The set up of the CEPT agency however indicates how strongly the post offices are committed to reorganising their services and operations to meet customer needs. The Express Mail Service (EMS) is a good case in point. Already EMS is growing at a phenomenal rate showing how well the post offices are rising to the new challenges in the marketplace.

Future Strategy

The post offices of Europe (and the world) are on the threshold of a radical change in their position towards global economy. Their precise role in this will be determined by the needs of the information society, the opportunities presented by communications technology, the commercialisation of state and semi-state enterprises and the increasing intensity of competition.

Direct marketing will be a key to business and consumer communication in the information society of the future. Currently over 10 billion addressed direct mail pieces are posted every year in Europe. This total will continue to grow as direct mail develops further and countries with underdeveloped direct mail markets catch up. The post offices of the future will also have to think increasingly as one is planning and developing new and existing services for business customers.

Governments, customers and Post Office personnel all expect and demand that the post organisation be more commercial both in their attitudes as well as in their policies in order to play a fully active role in a more competitive marketplace. The rest of this chapter summarises facts regarding population, number of households and growth in mail order for 12 SEM countries.

A Summary of Direct Mail and Postal Services in the 12 SEM Countries

TABLE 1
The Twelve SEM Countries

1. Belgium	7. Netherlands
2. Denmark	8. Norway
3. Finland	9. Portugal
4. France	10. Sweden
5. Germany	11. Switzerland
6. Ireland	12. United Kingdom

Belgium

For details of growth in Direct Mail, number of direct marketing agencies, specialist list brokers/owners, other list sources and direct marketing associations refer to Ref 3. Robinson lists do not exist in Belgium. A self-regulating system is implied in code of address in list holders. It permits names and addresses from the list of affiliated companies. The Belgian Post Office and Postal Cheque Service is an independent state enterprise; together they offer the direct marketer an impressive range of direct mail services.

Methods of despatch: Letter, postogram, printed matter, magazines, small parcels and advertising samples, non-addressed (door-to-door) advertising mail, preferential rates for pre-sorting, regular bulk mailings.

Replies: Postage paid by addressee, business reply, coded messages on payment forms.

Express Service: Express mailpost, datapost, bureaufax.

Franking: Stamps, franking machines, cash payment (postage paid) PP—PB.

International Business Reply Service: Belgium co-operates in the IBRS together with 13 other Western European countries. The charge made for replies is that of prevailing rates for international letter postage.

Belgium is an exporting country and ideally situated at the communications crossroads of Europe (the international seaport of Antwerp; Brussels as the centre of the EECL; NATO headquarters).

Contact Belgian Post Office, Post-Info, Muntcenter, Muntplein, B—1000 Brussels.

Tel: 32 (0) (2) 219.38.60 extension 1078/79

For postal rates and detailed mailing information for Belgium and abroad:

Postal Cheque Service, International Department, WTC2, 1000 Brussels.

Tel: 32 (0) (2) 218.22.96

For letter and postcards, postogram, printed matter, parcels and promotional samples, franking and processing replies, more detail is given in Ref 3.

Privacy regulations and consumer protection legislation — so far Belgium has no legislaltion on consumer privacy protection. At the moment, a bill is under discussion in parliament. This bill will relgulate various aspects of personal privacy, including data protection. Export Regulations, Customs and VAT. Operating internationally becomes easier when Post Office and customer are under the same roof. Commercial services of the Belgium Post Office can provide full addresses of these centres in: Brussels, Antwerp, Charlerio, Mons, Gent, Liege, Namur.

Contact Address: Regie des Postes Belges Service Commercial 1.4. Centre Monnaie. B—1000 Brussels.

Tel: 32 (0) (2) 219.38.60 extension 1078/79 Contacts Mr A Trogh, L Dujardin, M Matheus, R Laeman

Denmark

List sources: The main sources are companies which own and rent compiled lists — primarily business lists — although a limited number of private consumer list are available. Lists available in accordance with ISIC codes and it is possible to segment them by postal code, company turnover and employee numbers. Turnover and employee numbers are available only, for larger companies. Denmark has over 400,000 companies of which only 20,000 have large enough turnovers. These companies represent 80% of total turnover. Address lists are supplied on tape, as labels or on cards. Telephone numbers are available of decision makers for a number of larger companies.

Business lists are also available from Government Statistical Department. Consumer lists are scarce. An amount of "list swapping" occurs between non-competing mail order suppliers. Lists are normally rented on a one-time basis, but special terms can be agreed for repeat usage. Lists are purchased from the Government Statistical Department.

A Robinson list has not, as yet been established in Denmark.

Direct Marketing/Direct Mail Organisations: The Danish Marketing Association has a special working committee which organises lectures, conferences, seminars, educational courses on direct marketing. Contact: DANSK MARKEDSFORING-SFIRBUND, Vesterbrogade 24, KD—1620 Copenhagen V. Telephone 01/224688.

Mail order suppliers have a membership organisation of 47 members at August 1988. Ref 3 lists all these names and addresses.

Mail order suppliers have a membership of approximately 50 members, some of which are listed in Ref 3.

Danish Postal Service offers two channels of distribution for users of direct mail: addressed mail and unaddressed mail. Discounts on addressed mail when mailing a minimum of 10,000 items, franked or PP marked, postal codes must be included in all addresses and mailings must be delivered to a single Post Office. Additional discounts are allowed when mailings are sorted and bundled for direct to at least 40 local post offices. Business reply cards can be included in both addressed and non-addressed mailings. Further information on design and requirements for use of the business reply service can be obtained from the Danish Postal Service. Further details on "goneaways" privacy and Direct Mail Awards is given in Ref 3.

Finland

Information on direct mail letters, addressed bulk mail, non-addressed bulk mail is given in Ref 3. Non-addressed bulk mail can be delivered to the following groups:

Addresses	Total Finland
Households	2,138,000
Farmers	171,000
Detached Houses	1,111,000
Apartments	823,000
Student Apartments	38,000
Apartments for the Aged	36,000
Companies	135,000
Shops	44,000
P O Boxes	44,000

Non-addressed bulk mail is delivered in 3 days. Faster distribution at a higher rate. The business reply service is available for inland Mail, mail to Scandinavian countries and to 10 other European countries. Address lists are available from the Post Office. To speed up handling, addresses are given in postal code sequence order. Finland has a Robinson list containing names which do not wish to receive direct mail advertising. Almost all advertising agencies in Finland handle direct marketing campaigns. There are also specialised direct mail agencies and fulfilment houses. Further information on lists etc can be obtained from Direct Marketing Association of Finland, telephone — 358 0 498542, address: Frederikink 58A SF — 00100 Helsinki, Finland.

Details of protection legislation is detailed in Ref 3. For further details contact: The Office of Data Protection Ombudsman, PO Box 31, SF—00931, Helsinki, Finland, Telephone — 358 0 3432455. Door-to-door and mail order sale of consumer goods (selected parts) is given in Ref 3.

France

During the five year period 1982—87, direct mail expenditure increased by 84%. The major institutions in direct marketing are listed and discussed in Ref 3. The SEVPCD (Syndicat des Enerprises de Vente par Correspondence et à Distance) represents the interest of mail order companies engaged in mail order sales. Set up in 1957 the SEVPCD is the national association of mail order firms and represents about 90% of all direct mail business volume in France. Only mail order companies can become members, other companies can become associate members. Objectives and the professional code are detailed in Ref 3. The Association regularly sends its members a list of people not wishing to receive direct mail. Services of the association can be obtained from: SEVPCD, 60 Rue de la Boétie, 75008, Telephone (1) 42 56 3886. The Advertising Consultants Association can be contacted at ASCC, 40 Boulevard Malesherbes 75009 Paris, telephone (1) 47 42 13 42. Subscription and Direct Mail Fulfilment established in 1969 is described in Ref 3 and can be contacted at MAP, 46 Rue de Bassano, 75008, Paris, telephone (1) 20 45 90. Union Des Announceurs (UDA) the advertisement association can be contacted at UDA, Union Des Announceurs, 53 Rue Victor Hugo, 75116, Paris, telephone (1) 45 00 79 10. The Telemarketing Association can be contacted at Syndicat due Marketing Teléphonique, 4 Rue de Commailee, 75007 Paris, telephone (1) 46 08 38 38.

Postal services with details of price and all forms of direct mail postage is available in Ref 3. France co-operates with 15 other countries in the International Business Reply Service.

Privacy regulations and consumer protection details are given in Ref 3. Under an Act (January 1978) the CNIL (Commission Nationale Informatique et Liberties) has laid down a number of principles in respect of the protection of privacy.

Germany

In 1987 household and businesses received a total of 4,000 million direct mail items (including 670 million non-addressed printed mail). Direct mail has grown by 20% in the eight year period 1980/87 which means an average growth rate of about 2.5% on a yearly basis.

In Germany, most companies involved in direct marketing are members of the Deutscher Direct Marketing Verband (DDV) Schiersteiner Str. 29, 6200 Wieskaden, telephone 06121/84 30 61. Members whose names/addresses are given include:

Advertising Agency Consultants (87)

Printer and Manufacturers (46)

List Brokers, Fulfilment Enterprises, Lettershops (52)

Users of Direct Marketing (48)

Door-to-door Distribution Companies (40)

Tele-marketing Companies (47)

Applications for inclusion in the Robinson list are handled by the Association. The above applies to W.Germany before and upon unification. New arrangements can be obtained from Ref 3.

Details of mailing arrangements for the unified Germany should be sought prior to embarking upon a mailing.

Republic of Ireland

The volume of direct mail in 1988 was in excess of 20 million items. Direct Mail accounted for a small percentage of the total amount spent on all advertising media in 1988. However, growth can be measured by the fact that spending on An Post's direct mail services more than doubled between 1985 and 1988.

Mailing lists are available from various sources. For details of list brokers and list management/owner contact: Field Sales Manager, General Post Office, O'Connel Street, Dublin 1, Ireland.

The Irish Marketing Association has been operating since the end of 1989. This is a self regulatory representative of the industry and users. Further details can be obtained by contacting the address above.

An Post has developed the following targeting and response services that are effective and accessible to both small and large advertisers:

POSTAIM, the market can be targeted and achieve good value for money and postaim rates can be as little as half the price of a standard seated letter. Sample post is also dealt with as is unaddressed mail which can reach everybody without addressing. Publicity Post offers low cost blanket coverage for any chosen country.

A good direct response service is available. Freepost and International Business Reply Service is available to 14 countries in Europe. Parcel Forward Service, National Services, Printed Paper Service, Registered Service, Airmail letters/small packet, Accelerated Bulk Service, Surface Bulk Service and insurance details are provided in Ref 3 along with other details.

The Netherlands

Direct Mail accounted for nearly 21% of all spending on advertising in 1990. PTT post supplies various address lists drawn from a public file, as are over 4 million names and address of private individuals who have a telephone.

A wide range of consumer business lists are available. Standard conditions for list rental are generally:

- lists normally only available on a single user per-rental basis
- list owners reserve the right to agree or decline to rent lists to any organisation and/or for any promotion

- list owners may demand a sample mailing piece before releasing the list
- list users are generally prohibited from using a rental list other than for the purpose expressly agreed between renter and owner.

Mailing lists are based on Demographic Profiling Systems. The system has interesting applications:

- Market Segmentation:
- social-economic profiles
- allocation target group
- Customer investigation:
- market investigation
- prospect files

For more information about the systems, contact: Geo. Marktprofiel, National Institnut voor Markgerietite, Post-codesgmentatie, Weerdestein 205, 1083 Amsterdam, telephone 020—461046.

In the Netherlands most companies involved in Direct Marketing are members of the Netherlands Direct Marketing Institute — their main objectives are given in Ref 3. The Dutch Robinson list (known as Reply Number 666) was introduced by the above institute. All details of postal services can be obtained from: PTT Post B V. Product Moneyement, P O Box 30250, 2500 GG The Hague.

An appendix in Ref 3 Netherlands lists 23 agencies for business addresses, and 91 agencies for consumer addresses.

Norway

Direct mail advertising currently accounts for 30% of the total advertising market and is constantly growing. A consumer survey carried out in 1985 into what the public thought of receiving advertising material by post revealed the following:

- 19% took a positive attitude to receiving advertising material by post
- 78% normally read/glanced at the material
- 47% had made use of mail order firms

Post Office services can be obtained by contacting Oslo Postterminal, Brevavdelgen, N—0220 Oslo 1, Norway.

Within Norway unaddressed items may be sent to the following categories of addresses:

- Households
- Apartments in villas/small apartment house
- shops and Offices
- Farmers

Information on a data medium or in the form of pre-printed labels can be obtained from: POSTDIREKTORET, POST-VERKETS, DATASENTRAL, Postboks 1191 Sentrium, N0107 Oslo 1, Norway. Questions on Norwegian EDP legislation may be directed to the Data Inspectorate at DATA-TILSYNET, Postboks 8177 DP, N—24, Oslo 1, Norway, telephone — 02 44 70 22.

A licence is needed for the establishment of:

- Databased personal records
- Manual personal records containing sensitive data
- Credit information services
- Data processing enterprises
- Addressing and distribution services
- Public opinion poll measurements
- Market analysis

Application forms can be obtained from the Data Inspectorate.

Portugal

Direct mail only started in the early 1980's but has picked up relatively strongly in the last few years as the basis and structure of the industry starts to become delineated. The volume of direct mail in 1988 was 90.4 million items. In the period 1983—88, volume increased by 58.5%.

Currently only 4 firms specialise in business lists and one on consumer lists.

In 1989, there were only 3 direct marketing agencies. There are no mailing houses or lettershops and as yet no direct mail organisation.

The Portuguese Post Office has been working hard to encourage direct mail. Strong demand from the market place for such services has given a strong impulse to direct mail. For first time users the Post Office handles free of charge, the first 3000 items of any direct mail campaign.

Reply Paid Business Cards (RSP) paid by the sender per reply received. Most contain certain indications of the cost of the printed matter.

Five names/addresses of business lists supplied in Portugal are given in Ref 3 and three Direct Marketing Agencies are listed.

Sweden

Direct Mail's share of the total advertising market in 1988 increased by 30% compared with 1987.

In Sweden four different postal categories are used for direct mail with rates variable depending on needs in terms of speed, delivery, exclusiveness, price and volume. Normal letter is the most expensive and delivery is the next day. These are economy letters and addressed bulk mailings. (Mass letters) is the most common type of direct mail vehicle. There are four types of Business Reply Service. Details of postal rates and privacy regulations can be obtained by contacting: Swedish Direct Marketing Organisation, Box 14038, S—10440 Stockholm, Telephone 08 661 39 10 and for postal administration: Sweden Post, Letters and Parcels Mr Torbjorm Karlsson, S—10500 Stockholm, Telephone 08 7817479.

Switzerland

In 1988, 1336 million items of addressed and unaddressed direct mail were distributed by the Swiss PTT throughout the country, an increase of 22% for the 5 year period 1983—88. In 1987 Swiss advertisers spent on addressed and unaddressed direct mail 37% of the total spent on all forms of advertising.

Direct mail is, together with advertising in newspapers and magazines, the most important advertising media in Switzerland. Each year the postal service handles about 600 million pieces of addressed direct mail which represents approximately 25% of letter post traffic.

Post/Delivery rules and prices on all items can be obtained from:

Mailings in Switzerland:	International Mailings:
PTT General Directorate	PTT General Directorate
Postal Operations	International Affairs
Customer Service	CH 303 Bern
CH — 3030 Bern	Tel: 031/62 44 19
Tel: 031/62 52 09 or 62 38 24	

Business reply cards/envelopes need to conform to certain design specifications. Practically unlimited advertising on address side. International Business Reply Systems (IBRS) is one of the participants in the trial service IBRS. Brochures, leaflets and folders with detailed information on Swiss PTT services/rates are available in German, French or Italian and obtained from PTT General Directorate as well as from each local customer service department.

The address of the Direct Marketing Association is given in Ref 3 and 58 names/addresses of members with business code and a contact address of mail order houses is also given. A Robinson list is maintained by the Swiss Direct Marketing Association. Import/export regulations will be supplied by General Directorate of Swiss Customs, Monbijoustr, 40, 3000 Bern. Telephone 031/61 11. Customer protection legislation —Switzerland has none of the protection of consumer privacy, but a bill is under discussion at the time of writing.

United Kingdom

In the past five years, the volume of direct mail has grown by just over 50%, as has expenditure on direct mail postage and production.

A wide variety of business lists are available in the UK whether response, enquirer, subscription or compile based.

There are four main types of UK operators involved in the provision, servicing of lists;

The List Owner owns the list and makes it available for rental.

The List Manager is responsible for management and servicing. This involves promotion to users, rental negotiation and organisation, file maintenance and accounting. The list manager may be employed by the list owner or retained by the owner on a commission basis.

The List Broker acts for the list user and uses his professional knowledge and experience to recommend lists to users and advises them on availability, history and track record, for reaching specific audiences. List brokers are remunerated by list owners on a commission basis.

The Computer Bureaux acting either for owner or user, provide the necessary processing services such as formulating and duplicating. Questions to ask when renting a list in the UK are noted in Ref 3 and relate to matters in the previous section on list brokers. For advice and access to the Consumer Location System contact: Direct Mail Sales Bureau, 14 Floral Street, London WC2E 9RR, telephone 071–379 7531.

"Lister " (Life Style Evaluation Report) is a Post Office development aimed at increasing the effectiveness of list selection and marketing in the direct mail industry through the use of research-based techniques.

Post coding and other details can be obtained from: Post Code Consultancy Service, Postal Headquarters, 33 Grosvenor Place, London SW1X 1PX, telephone 071–245 7360.

The Robinson list is a free service for UK consumers (not businesses). Companies can obtain information from Mailing Preference Service, 26 Eccleston Street, London SW1W 9PY, telephone 071–730 0869.

Ref 3 gives names/addresses of British List Brokers Association (BLBA), British Direct Marketing Association, Direct Mail Producers Association, Direct Mail Services Standards Board and the Advertising Standards Authority.

REFERENCES

1. Royal Mail, The Complete Package, Finding International Business, Getting Customers to Respond, Delivering the Goods.
2. Royal Mail SPE Service Guide to European Direct Mail, 1989.
3. Royal Mail International Mailing Lists, How to Use Them, Where to Find Them.
4. Royal Mail Intentional (RM) Headquarters, 52 Grosvenor Gardens, London SW1W 1AA.
5. Royal Mail Intentional, Business Travel Guide, 1st Edition 1990/91 Columbus Press, 384 page book.
6. Royal Mail International, Airstream (Package).
7. Royal Mail International, Printflow, 10 page brochure with photographs.
8. Royal Mail International, Price and Services, 18 page brochure.
9. Royal Mail International, International Business Reply Service, 4 page brochure PL (B) 4472 (LB) 9/90.
10. The Royal Mail Direct Mail Handbook, 2nd Edition, 1988.

FURTHER READING

1. Bird, D. Commonsense Direct Marketing 1988, Wyvern Business Library, Ely. Cambs CB7. 4BR.
2. Jefkins, Frank. The Secrets of Successful Direct Response Marketing, 1988. Heinemann Professional Publishing Limited.
3. Booth, D. Principles of Strategic Marketing, chapters 5, 6, 7. Tudor Business Publishing 1990.

CHAPTER 13

SOURCES OF ASSISTANCE FOR EXPORTERS

Introduction

The purpose of this chapter is to identify the various sources of assistance available to exporters, and to summarise the contents of the literature available from a wide variety of sources. Hopefully this will save many hours of research by those wishing to devise a communication strategy which will enable their organisations to engage successfully in international trade either with the EC or the rest of the world.

The British Overseas Trade Board (BOTB) Publication

"Help for Exporters — Now's the time to Export" gives a summary of all the services provided by the BOTB with appropriate addresses and telephone numbers.

The statistics and market intelligence library provides access to a wide and thorough collection of foreign statistics, trade directories, development plans and other published information on overseas markets. The library is open to personal users Monday to Friday from 9.30 am to 5.30 pm. Further information and short enquiries by telephone can be dealt with at:

The Statistic and Market Intelligence Library
1 Victoria Street
London SW1 OET
Telephone 071–215 5444/5

The Product Data Store also at the above address provides a cental "bank" of product and industry based information about markets nationwide. A leaflet, 'Product Data Store', is available on request.

Market Advice is available to firms and individuals who do not know enough hard facts about their overseas market. A scheme is available to provide accurate market facts before decisions can be taken about making a sales effort.

The Export Marketing Research Scheme

- offers free professional advice on how to set about Market Research to the best advantage and;
- having decided on a market research project, give a grant of up to 50% towards the costs — up to a maximum of £20,000 can be given.

The booklet "Help for Exports" Export Marketing Research Scheme is available to provide further details to keep you up to date and the whole range of international opportunities through the BOTB monitoring service, the publication "Help for Exporters" — World Aid Section will be sent on request.

Getting into the Market — information to aid potential exporters who need to find a representative abroad can be obtained from the booklet "Export Representatives Service".

To explore working with a possible trading partner abroad, the booklet "Overseas Status Report Service" should be requested.

Appointing an agent or distributor abroad can be both successful and profitable, as the literature indicates. However it could also be perilous. This service can provide an impartial report on the agent or distributor's capability and commercial standing. Ventures into the market can be aided further by asking for information given in the publication "Export Intelligence Service" which deals with:

- Type of export information handled;
- Speed of Service;

- How items are categorised;
- Matching your interest to our categories;
- Different combinations for different needs and;
- Subscription rates.

Outward Missions. Whilst many missions overseas are run by Chambers of Commerce or Trade Associations, the BOTB can help a firm to join a mission and explore at first hand the prospects for its product. The new exporter will benefit from contact with more experienced members of the mission. Firms can learn about the practical advantages of joining a BOTB supported trade mission by reading the leaflet entitled "Outward Missions — Help for Exporters" from the nearest BOTB regional office and it gives details of new missions. The leaflet covers:

- How missions are organised;
- Countires included and excluded;
- Rates of grant and;
- Conditions for participants.

Those firms who may be put off by the complications and expense of exhibiting abroad can obtain help and advice from the BOTB whose leaflet "Trade Fairs Overseas" details:

- How BOTB support works;
- What is provided and the cost;
- Travel grants;
- British pavillions;
- All British exhibitions and;
- Conditions for participants.

The BOTB also supports specialised seminars abroad and gives generous help with costs as explained in its leaflet "Overseas Seminars — Help for Exporters".

Further publications available for exporters (including aid for getting into the market) is available in: "Store Promotions — Help for Exporters" which gives advice on:

- Where to find out about promotions;
- How to offer your products;

- Timing and buying season;
- Main locations and;
- The role of the BOTB.

Participating in a well organised promotions event can often help the ambitious firm to enter a new market, or expand it's business if it's there already.

Firms often wish to influence visitors (opinion leaders?) from abroad to show what they can supply. The BOTB can help bring the right people to Britain and put a firm on their itinerary. The leaflet "Inward Missions — Help for Exporters" is available by contacting the regional BOTB office.

Specialist advice and help from the BOTB is available through specialist staff who handle them full time and can supply information on:

- Import duties
- Local taxes
- Import licensing regulations
- Import restrictions
- Temporary importation

- Foreign investment and manufacturing under licence
- Agency legislation
- Custom procedures

- Documentation
- Samples
- Free zones

- Price control
- Marketing and labelling of goods
- Transport

- Weights and measures
- Regulations covering dangerous goods
  eg.
    — drugs and medicines
    — foodstuffs
    — livestock
    — spirits, wines, beers

The client firm should then contact the nearest BOTB Market Branch to handle its enquiry. If that branch cannot answer the query, it will put the enquirer in touch with the specialist who can.

Under the heading "Specialist Advice and Help", other BOTB publications are suggested. They are:
"Technical Help for Exporters" which covers:

- Enquiry service
- Research and consultancy
- Up-dating services
- Technical translation
- Publications, and
- Fees

An important leaflet "SITPRO2, Simplification of International Trade Procedures — help for Exporters lists:

- Service available
- Documentation system
- Computers in international trade
- Savings on procedures
- Training materials
- Free management checklist and other publications.

SITPRO helps to create a cost-effective international trading environment and was established in 1970 as an independent agency supported by the DTI. SITPRO, the Simplification of Trade Procedures Board, has one prime objective — to make British companies more competitive in world trade. It is achieved by attacking red tape, developing the skills of the people involved and encouraging the use of information technology in the trading, distribution and payment process. This means:

- seeking the abolition of bureaucratic procedures;
- simplifying the process and attendant paperwork;
- developing Electronic Data Interchange (EDI) standards and the replacement of documents by EDI message sets;
- raising awareness of how EDI can be of benefit to companies and;
- advising on training and providing guidance.

To obtain further information, contact:

SITPRO
Venture House
29 Glashouse Street
London
Telephone 071–287 3525
Fax 071–289 5751
Further information on SITPRO's activities, products or services can be obtained by contacting this address.

The BOTB can assist in large scale operations through a special division that brings together all the various government support measures. These projects will normally offer a UK element in excess of £20m.

The Projects and Export Policy Division (PEP) of the BOTB provides a single focus for coordinating the full range of Government services available to support companies pursuing major international projects. PEP is divided into three branches all located at 1 Victoria Street, London SW1H OET, telephone ext. 8811074 and telephone enquiries are as follows:

Branch 1

Airports and equipment, canals, bridges, tunnels, roads 071–215 4914. Railways, trucks, shipyards, ports, transport system 071–215 4863

Branch 2

Hydroelectric and other alternative forms of energy production cement plant 071–215 4906. Chemical, petrochemical and other process plant 071–214 4904. Mining, all power products in India, defence 071–215 4910

Branch 3

Telecommunications, postal services, electronics, educational equipment projects 071–215 4855. Agricultural projects, fisheries, forestry, construction projects, water and sewerage 071–215 4843. Oil and gas (exploration, production, refining, distribution, pipelines) industrial projects, 071–215 4843.

Thermal generation and electrical distribution projects are the responsibility of the DTI's ship building and electrical engineering division, telephone 071–215 4843.

The British Overseas Board was set up in January 1972 to help British exporters. Its members come mainly from industry and commerce and are experienced in exporting. Government departments are also represented. The President is the Secretary of State for Trade and Industry. The Board's responsiblities are:

- To advice the Government on strategy for overseas trade;
- To direct and develop the Government export promotion service on behalf of the Secretary of State for Trade and Industry;
- To encourage and support industry and commerce in overseas trade with the aid of the appropriate governmental and non-governmental organisations at home and overseas and;
- To contribute to the exchange of views between Government and industry and commerce in the field of overseas trade and to search for solutions to promblems

The above background summary is taken from the leaflet "Help for Exporters — A Summary of all Services by the British Overseas Trade Board for UK Exporters". This leaflet and the BOTB annual report can be obtained by contacting the BOTB Regional Office or writing to:

BOTB Marketing and Briefing Unit
Room 228
1 Victoria Street
London SW1H OET
Telephone 071–215 5222

The BOTB offers further help on overseas publicity problems. A copy of its "Publicity for Exporters" can be obtained from a regional office or by writing to them at the above address.

Some other publications available are listed in the above booklet as well as brief descriptions of other organisations complementary to those of the BOTB. The local BOTB office will advise which best help in particular problem areas. They include:

- Export Credits Guarantee Department
- The Defence Export Services Organisation
- Chambers of Commerce. A firm may contact the Association of British Chambers of Commerce (ABCC) at Sovereign House, 212A Shaftesbury Avenue, London WC2H 8EW, telephone 071–240 5831/6.
- The banks
- Trade associations
- Export houses
- The Export Buying Offices Association
- Freight forwarders
- Air couriers
- **The International Chamber of Commerce** publishes a range of booklets on payment and documentations including Documentary Credits, Incomers, Commercial Agency Agreements, Exchange Rate Risks, Rules for Collections. This organisation can be contacted at:

ICC United Kingdom
Centre Point
103 New Oxford Street
London WC1A 1QB
Telephone 071–240 5558

THE DEPARTMENT OF TRADE AND INDUSTRY:—
Literature available on this subject includes:
The Single Market — The Facts, 3rd Edition, an 87 page leaflet whose contents include:

- The Single Market Programme
- Freedom of establishment for the professionals
- EC deregulation — avoiding red tape
- Influencing decisions
- Standards testing and certification
- Food law
- Pharmaceutical

- Public
- Information technology
- Financial services
- Insurance/capital movements
- Company law
- Competition policy
- State subsidies
- EC/EFTA trade relations
- Environment policy
- Collaborative R and D
- Selling in the single market
- Advice for small and medium sized businesses
- Transport

The Single Market — an action checklist for businesses, 3rd edition is a 23 page brochure dealing with:
- Marketing
- Sales
- Distribution
- Production Development
- Finance
- Training, languages and recruitment
- Information technology
- Where can we go for help?
- Purchasing

The Export Marketing Research Scheme, guidelines and notes, comment on the Export Marketing Research Scheme (EMRS) which is administered by the Association of British Chambers of Commerce on behalf of the Department of Trade and Industry. The scheme is designed to help marketing research as an integral part of export strategy by facilitating the systematic collection, collating, evaluating and presentation of information upon which marketing decisions can be based. Certain conditions of eligibility have to be fulfilled. The scheme can offer free professional advice on how to set about export marketing research and aspiring exporters can telephone market research advisers for help and an explanation of what is on offer.

The scheme offers financial help, for those who undertake a project, in one of four forms:

a) Through a member of the firm who is qualified and experienced in research. The project is conducted in-house when half of essential travel costs, interpreter's fee and a daily allowance towards hotel and meal costs for one researcher during overseas field work is available. This support does not extend to research relating to European countries.

b) Those commissioning published market research will have up to a third of the cost paid.

c) Those purchasing published market research will have up to a third of the cost paid.

d) For trade associations commissioning research, or carrying it out in-house on behalf of members, up to three quarters of the cost will be paid.

Notes on the scheme together with application forms are provided. "Export Briefing, BOTB, Help for Exporters" DTI. This 31 page brochure deals with:

- Money for market research
- The DTI service card
- Export Representative Service
- Overseas status report service
- New products from British service
- Trade Fairs
- Seminars, Workshops — What's happening in the North West
- Outward mission
- Country new/grants

"The Export Initiative" a guide to exporting BOTB, January 1989 edition is a useful 30 page brochure in 5 sections entitled:

1. Ready to Export?
2. Exporters' Checklist
3. Doing the Groundwork
4. Contacting the Market

5. Doing Business

"Introducing the Enterprise Initiative", Revised Edition September 1989. The 36 page brochure notes on:
1. The Enterprise Initiative
2. The Single European Market
3. Business and the Environment
4. The Consultancy Initiative
5. The Marketing Initiative
6. The Business Planning Information
7. The Financial Information Initiative
8. The Quality, Design and Manufacturing Systems Initiative
9. The Research/Technology, Enterprise and Education Initiatives
10. Support Services
11. Other services for small firms and Regional Contacts

The information pack "Vital Statistics" can be obtained from the Business and Statistics Office in Newport, Gwent (1) and contains details of the location and services available from the Statistics and Market Intelligence Library (SMIL). The DTI's headquarters in London is available for public use and contains collections of statistics, foreign and UK directories, and development plans. Exporters can use the information for desk research on overseas markets. A visit here is recommended since it will save time and money on research abroad.

SMIL keeps a collection of published economic statistics from overseas countries on topics such as trade, production, price, employment and transport. Available also are trade figures statistics of imports/exports from every country worldwide. Trade statistics are a vital step in market analysis — a comparison between a country's production and export figures against those for its imports gives an indication of the market.

SMIL holds those UK statistical publications relevant to exporters covering such areas as trade, industrial production statistics and general economic indicators. Market research is aided by the availability of commercially produced surveys to supplement official statistics. Published market research can be used as a valuable time saver. Readers should check the indexes to find out if the information available on their special service is listed.

Directories of many links are available, with specialist directories covering particular sectors of industry. It is possible to obtain details of potential customers or competitors operating in specific commodity areas or countries where UK trade directories are not available.

Development plans are published by many countries and provide an indication of the current state of an economy and future projections. Newly published plans are advertised through the DTI's Export Intelligence Service and also in the magazine 'British Business'. Most of the plans are available for loan to exporters.

The DTI offers a wide range of services to exporters from a network of Regional Offices. Exporters should visit the product Data Store at 1—19 Victoria Street, London SW1H OET.

Enquiries on the Business Monitor Services and other UK statistics can be obtained by contacting the Business Statistics Office Library, Cardiff Road, Newport, Gwent NP9 1XG, telephone 0633 222973, telex 497122.

The DTI pack "Vital Statistics " includes booklets on :

- Business monitors, designed for businesses and providing statistics on manufacturing, energy, mining service and distribution industries — compiled by the Government's Statistics Office (GSO)
- Government Statistics — a brief guide is "Sources of Information 1988 Edition".
- A business Monitor Form which when completed can be returned to the Business Statistics Office.

The newspaper, "Single Market", is published in the spring, summer and autumn and will be sent by the DTI if readers contact the Regional Office.

Further valuable information in the booklet "Hints to Exporters" can be obtained by contacting the DTI Regional Office in the reader's area. For example:

Hints to Exporters, The Federal Republic of Germany and West Berlin.

Other booklets in the same series cover, France, Netherlands, Antilles and Arabia.

other details on publications/country profiles area available from DTI/BOTB such as:

Country Profile — France (66 pages)

Market Consumer Goods — France (75 pages)

With such a quantity of literature and help available, the exporter/importer in the UK is well placed to enter the single market.

Lastly, readers are advised to obtain from the DTI under its Enterprise Initiative literature details of the range of consultancy help available. The consultancy initiatives aim to increase a firm's competiveness by providing advice in certain key management functions. They help to prepare for the increased competition that will arise from the completion of the European Market by the end of 1992. The DTI booklet detailing these schemes is titled "Applications and Guidance Notes for Consultancy" dealing with marketing, design, quality, manufacturing systems. The Regional DTI Office will supply these or, the DTI's Single Market Campaign on the 1992 hotline (081–200 1992) can be used.

There is no shortage of up to date references and literature being issued at a great pace from the BOTB, DTI, banks and accounting firms. Some of the latest literature on the subject of internationlisation and going global includes some recent articles from Fortune Magazine, which may provide food for thought to those firms wishing to spread their wings abroad. These include:—

"How To Go Global — And Why" — Fortune 29 August 1989 (8)

This article attempts to answer the questions why and how to go global in summary Why? To survive. How? by looking at the whole world as one market. The firm is advised to buy, borrow, hire, and manufacture and gain local allies wherever they can do it best. This article further discusses a company without borders, ICI, and its major operations which readers may find educational.

Another publication which will be of particular interest to all companies wishing to make their services available in the single market is: "1992 — Strategies for the Single Market" by James W Dudley (11). It deals with:—

- Strategic management for the Single Market
- Inward opportunities and collaborative arrangements
- Market research
- Product and pricing strategies
- New product development strategies
- International advertising and media policies
- Physical distribution and customer service
- Threats and opportunities for domestic firms
- Competition from Japan, America, the Pacific Basin and Europe
- Foreign exchange
- Plans, timetables and budgets.

Major Banks

Useful information for individuals and firms wishing to export is available from major banks. Examples of brochures and leaflets available from National Westminster, Midland, TSB, and Barclays Bank, are noted below.

The National Westminster pamphlet (1) introduces its services for the exporters and importers by advising . . . "International trade today is taking place in an increasingly competitive and complex environment. If you are to achieve success in your international trade activities you will want the best advice available". Their brochure provides a list of publications available. These are:

- Guide for exporting and importing
- International movement of money
- Documentary credits
- Foreign bonds and guarantees
- Export insurance and finance
- International trade bulletins (published monthly)
- Foreign exchange for importers and exporters
- Foreign currency accounts explained

These can be obtained by completing a form and indicating the brochure required.

The following information is provided by the National Westminster Bank:

- Economic reports
- International trade bulletins
- Economic and financial outlook
- Overseas visits
- Trade opportunities
- Together with several other publications

As well as providing information, the National Westminster Bank also offers various services which importers and exporters could find invaluable, these services include:

- Documentary credits
- Advance payment/open account
- Bills for collection
- Cargo Insurance
- International Bonding

National Westminster Bank is a leader in the London Foreign Exchange and Money Markets, and for this reason has many specialist managers who can advise on and deliver currency and interest rate management services which cover topics from spot foreign exchange to currency options and financial futures.

The brochure includes the names, addresses and telephone numbers of some 20 banks.

Midland Bank provides help and information to importers and exporters (2). Their brochure lists services on offer which include:

- Documentary Credits
- Bills of exchange
- Foreign currency accounts
- Multi currency cheque accounts

This brochure, entitled Midland Services For Importers and Exporters (2) is available at High Street Branches and includes an enquiry form which can be used to order the following publications:

- Services for Importers
- Services for Exporters

Brochures from the TSB (3) and Barclays Bank, list the services that they offer, which include:

- Documentary credits
- Bills for collection
- Export Finance Scheme and ECGD facilities
- Foreign Exchange Services
  - - Foreign currency accounts
- Simple fund transfer
- Bonds, guarantees and indemnities

The TSB brochure concludes with a useful glossary of terms.

Two booklets of interest to both the importer and exporter are available from Barclays High Street Banks. These are Import/Export Funding and Merchanting (4) and Barclays Tradeline and Trade Flow short term export finance (5) published under International Trade Services.

Brochure (4) lists the addresses and telephoned numbers of seven commercial services offices. Further details of all services offered are available from:

Barclays Commercial Services Limited
Arbuttnot House
Breeds Place
Hastings
East Sussex
TN34 3DG
Tel. 0424 430824
Fax 0424 721361

Brochures on the following topics are also avilable from the above address:

- Domestic and International Factoring
- Invoices Discounting (confidential and disclosed)

CHAPTER 14

MARKET RESEARCH

Introduction

Communication with the market place is an essential aspect of any marketing effort, however for communication to be effective it must be two-way communication. It is essential that the marketing organisation obtains feedback from the market place regarding reaction to its marketing message and to its products or services.

This two-way communication process is achieved by a programme of market research. Market research is particularly important prior to the launch of a new product in order to establish that there is actually a potential demand for the product and if so what is the extent of that demand. The vital rule here is that no product should ever be launched purely on a hunch and great care should be taken to ensure that my perceived demand actually exists.

Definitions

Market research can be defined as: the process of systematic investigation into markets in order to:

- Establish present and potential demand for consumer and industrial products

and

- Provide a basis for management decisions.

Information from research reduces the element of uncertainty and thereby sets limits on the decisions which have to be made. Research undertaken needs to be sound and scientific i.e. logical in method and objective in outlook and it must be careful not to give a false sense of security. Judgement still has to be exercised in preference to guesswork. Many small companies have attempted superficial research and have used some optimistic "guesswork", with fatal results. Some firms have even employed researchers and then are reluctant to believe the results since they do not "fit in" with their ideas. This may be because the client company does not know its market, although it is possible that incorrect bases have been employed in the survey.

Market Research

Market research therefore attempts to clarify the organisation's understanding of the markets in which it operates. In order to do this it will require information in a number of key areas.

Market Size

- Number of customers
- Volume of purchases
- Expenditure

This information is required for both the market as it currently exists and what it is likely to be in the future based upon current trends.

Customer Characteristics

- Characteristics of the typical buyer
- Differences between buyers

Market Characteristics

- Level of current competition
- Rate of entry to the industry and future competition
- Competitor performance

Marketing Research

Marketing research is concerned with those variations which influence the market and can therefore be used to alter it, preferably in favour of our product or service. This involves seeking answers to questions such as:

- What motivates consumers to buy the product?
- How much will consumers pay for the product?
- How and where do they normally buy it?
- Why is it preferred to competitors products?
- How did the consumer find out about the product?

Analysis should then concentrate on how well our organisations marketing effort is responding to these factors and whether are competitors are performing any better.

The Marketing Research Process

For marketing research to be conducted effectively it must be conducted in a systematic manner. The stages in the process are as follows.

- Problem definition and setting objectives
- Establishing the plan for research
- Data collection
- Presentation of findings and recommendations for action

This can be illustrated as a systems approach to management information in the flow diagram below.

Diagram 1

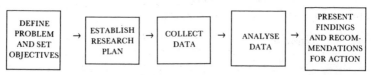

Defining our problem and setting objectives at the outset is essential, as with any expensive research, as we need to be crystal clear as to what we are trying to achieve. Failure to do this may be at least costly or at worst a disaster for the organisation if it acts upon a false premise.

Sources of Information

Sources of information can include the firm's own sales statistics and information published by competitors and Trade Associations. Government statistics can provide useful sources of information although some care is necessary in using this source in terms of the need to check definitions carefully. Many general publications such as newspapers, The Economist and trade journals provide further sources.

Interviews of many types provide detailed information on needs, preferences and perceptions. These may take the form of:

- Personal interviews carried out by independent consultants or interviewers from a specialist agency.
- Group interviews and discussion which can be very useful in ascertaining attitudes.
- Consumer panels. Members of such panels need to be changed frequently for a number of obvious reasons.
- Telephone surveys are popular, particularly in the U.S.A., for consumer surveys. Often a telephone call may be used to discover if a visit would be worthwhile.

Surveys by post can be unsuccessful since they may be dealt with by someone of little importance and without suitably detailed knowledge. Many questionnaires are thrown in the waste paper basket, whilst others get an irrelevant reply.

It is worthwhile at this point distinguishing between industrial and consumer market research.

Consumer Research

Consumer research is used in the highly competitive consumer market for foodstuffs, soap powders, cosmetics, toothpastes etc. Only a small sample of consumers can be questioned and the sample must therefore be statistically representative. Questions asked are normally predetermined and fixed for the

survey. Attitudes may be tested as well as buying characteristics. Such goods are classified as Fast Moving Consumer
Goods (F.M.C.G.'s)

Industrial Research

The number of businesses in an industry are relatively limited,
and purchasers of equipment and materials are generally
experienced and knowledgeable in the trade. These circumstances call for quite a different approach to that followed for
consumer research. Information is obtained by personal interview and the interviewer must be experienced, able to ask
relevant questions, and note pertinent data which may be
revealed in the course of the meeting. Much relevant information
can be obtained from other sources, but care must be exercised to
keep within the terms of reference. Such terms must be clear and
specify whether, for instance, all products of a class are to be
examined or only one; one market or all markets.

As stated earlier problem definition is a preliminary statement
of the research objectives which normally requires the collection
of substantial amounts of information in order to establish an
outcome. The information is to be found from two sources.
Secondary data sources from outside and inside the firm, and
Primary data sources obtained from "fieldwork".

The information needed may be very broad but will
generally be about products, brands, companies, retail stores,
service and charitable organisations as well as about individuals. Information needed may relate to:

- Opinions
- Values
- Beliefs
- Motivation

- Attitudes
- Intentions
- Knowledge
- Behaviour

- Lifestyle
- Social grades
- Minority groups

Secondary Source Data is available from:

- Company records and previous research findings
- Research organisations and government departments,
  trade and professional organisations
- Market research agencies

- Trade/professional conferences, seminars
- Technical literature, periodicals, government statistics, newspapers

New or Primary Information will be obtained through:

- Surveys by personal interview, telephone or post
- Observation and experimentation
- Motivational research methods from in-depth interviewing and group discussion/interviewing.

As discussed above, the data following collection is analysed, results evaluated and recommendations for action made.

Field Research

Field and laboratory experiments are used to evaluate the affect of changes in the product or service, its price, type of packaging, outlet or method of advertising and promotion. Controlled field experiments calculate the change in resulting sales arising from changes in these variables. Laboratory experiments provide a controlled method of determining the effect of price, packaging and other stimuli on individual consumers, groups or panels. Whilst laboratory tests are somewhat artificial, valuable information can be made available to suppliers of goods in terms of measured attitudes to the product, price, packaging, advertising and promotion compared with competing products. Such tests provide an indication of customer reactions in the market place.

Selective observations of people sometimes using mechanical devices can provide valuable insights into behaviour, although not to motivations. Observations in shops, children's reactions to toys or clothes, provides information on attitudes, preferences and intentions. As interviews are not conducted however there may be problems associated with the interpretation of observations. Mechanical devices such as eye cameras, which measure changes in pupil size, can measure interest and reactions to adverts. A tachistoscope, a projection device to present visual stimuli for a brief period, can be used to measure brand-name awareness. The use of tape recordings of discussions between sales staff and customers, the use of movie cameras and video tapes can all provide valuable research data. The use of traffic counters and television and radio audimeters are other examples of physical phenomena observed by mechanical devices.

Physical phenomena observed by people include the use of retail audits, "pantry" audits, information on brand stock levels. Products and brands on hand also provide basic information for the supplier company.

Survey Work-Methods

Surveys using questionnaires are widely used – and often abused. Surveys may be carried out by mail, telephone or personal interview and the method used will be dependent on type of information sought, amount of information needed, cost, accuracy required and the ease of questioning. The decision will require the determination of sample size, and the method of analysing results.

In surveys by mail the following should be considered:

- Who is the respondent? Industrial buyer, consumer, professional adviser?
- Will motivation to respond be high?
- What will be the length of the questionnaire and will it be simple to complete?
- What sample size is required?
- If a rented or purchased list is used, how up to date and accurate is it?
- Will a reply device be enclosed?
- What will be the response rate?

The covering letter will be important and ask for co-operation and possibly give instruction and guidance.

A good response provides a relatively low cost method of data collection but the speed of response may be slow and reminders may be necessary to speed up and increase response.

For telephone surveys similar considerations will apply and

this topic is further discussed in Chapter 5. The telephone is increasingly used as a relatively quick and cheap method of communicating with the prospect but suffers from the disadvantage of being impersonal and usually only permits speaking to one person when the respondent cannot consult other people and company records etc. Personal interviews are usually associated with high cost and discussed more fully in Chapter 5.

The respondent may be interviewed in the home, office, in the street or in a theatre queue. Factors affecting motivation to participate in an interview are numerous but will generally include:

- Pressure of competing activities, embarrassment or ignorance, fear of consequences, invasion of privacy
- Liking for the interviewer, interest in the content, loneliness, the prestige of the research agency.

Questionnaires

The preparation of a questionnaire requries considerable skill and in industrial selling often a good deal of technical knowledge. Too many open-ended questions will invite many responses and make analysis difficult. Questions may be structured – Yes/No, multiple choice, rankings or paired comparisons. In wording questions it is important to avoid ambiguity so that the questions means exactly the same to all respondents. The respondent's ability to answer depends on his or her education and language, and he or she may exhibit an unwillingness to answer blunt questions on personal matters.

In posing questions it is necessary to use language that does not influence the answer. In sequencing questions the initial questions need to be designed to provide motivation and encourage co-operation. There is a need for a logical order, from general to specific and the rotation of questions and subquestions will eliminate bias. Personal questions may be left to the end or inserted in the middle when appropriate. Questionnaire design should consider the following points:

- Does each question relate to the research objectives?
- Ensure that the form of the question does not influence the response
- Where closed-end questions are used allow the respondent to select from a range of responses, for example multiple choice questions.
- Ensure that some open-ended questions are included which allow respondents to answer in their own words
- Use clear, simple words, avoiding jargon and confusing, unecessary long words.
- Ensure that the sequence of the questions does not "lead" the respondent towards a desired conclusion
- Always ensure that the questionnaire is pre-tested with a sample group in order to eliminate any problems prior to the full test.

For example if the carpet cleaning company, Punters, used as an illustration in the earlier chapters wanted to find out market information regarding carpet cleaning services and asked the following questions:

1. Would you like to have clean carpets?   ————
2. How much would you pay for the services of a high quality carpet cleaning service?   ————

The answer to question 1 is highly unlikely to be no, hence this is an example of a leading question. In answer to question 2 respondents may well have no idea regarding the value of such services. These questions would be better posed in the following manner:

1. Do you currently use the services of a carpet cleaning company?   Yes ☐   No ☐
2. How much would you be prepared to pay for a carpet cleaning service?   LESS THAN £20 ☐
                                       £20–£30 ☐
                                       £30–£40 ☐
                                       £40–£50 ☐

Question 1, is an example of a dichotomous question, offering two answer choices, whilst Question 2 is a multiple choice

question which offers a range of responses. Open-ended questions should be used when there is a desire to elicit further information from respondents. For example:
What is your opinion of the services offered by Punters Carpet Cleaners? ————————————————————————

This is an example of an unstructured open-ended question. Alternative types of open-ended question include sentence completion questions and word associations.

Questionnaires can be a vital source of information but can be highly misleading if not well designed in the first instance, hence time and effort at this stage pays dividends later.

Motivated Research Techniques

Motivated research techniques try to find the underlying motives, desires and emotions of consumers that relate to their behaviour. The techniques penetrate below the level of the conscious mind and uncover motives which consumers are not aware of or tend to hide. Two approaches to motivated research are:

a) The psychoanalytical approach. This technique relies on what is drawn from individuals in depth interviews and projective tests.
b) The psychosociological approach relies on group behaviour of consumers and the impact of culture and environment on their opinions and reactions.

The techniques used are:

Depth Interviewing

Depth interviewing uses interviewing and observational methods. The interviewer chooses topics for discussion and through non-structured indirect questions, leads the respondent to free expression of motives, attitudes, opinions, experience and habits in relation to adverts, products, brands, services etc.

Group Interviewing

Group interviewing techniques are those where the interviewer stimulates and moderates group discussion to encourage freedom of expression and interaction between individuals.

Projective Techniques

Here the respondent sometimes reveals what he or she may cover up in direct questioning. Verbal projectives may seek answers to questions such as "What do you think people do in a situation . . .?" When a person is asked about someone else, their answer may reveal their own view. Other methods use word association tests, response to pictures, and sentence completion of the type "people buy on credit when . . ."

Use of Outside Agencies

Marketing texts and most sources of advice on the subject stress the importance of thoroughly researching the market for the firm's products or services before their launch. Market research is a scientific business which can be carried out most effectively by skilled and experienced professionals. The use of outside specialists, in addition to ensuring that the research is thorough, should also ensure that the research is unbiased. This help can be expensive for the smaller firm. A prestigious research company (1) gives some examples of the type of work undertaken with an indication of cost. Three examples given by the firm are summarised below:

1. How do I define and forecast my markets, improve marketing strategy?
    Executive intreviews with competitors and end-users was undertaken. The report showed present and projected market size and segments, company and product image versus competition, competitor policies and future product/service developments. The report set out realistic targets, and the sales and product development strategy (or acquisition strategy) with priorities for action. £12–18,000.

2. How do I find and develop new markets quickly from an open brief?

   The research company worked successfully with the client to generate a list of new product ideas, surveyed them by desk research and telephone enquiries, then carried out interviews at a high level amongst companies operating in the promising markets. The report concentrated on product design and marketing methods for the best products. £12–16,000.

3. Is my product or service right for the market?

   Through group discussions, telephone and individual interviews, the research company found out how the product or service was chosen, what features appealed and how it should be designed and presented. A detailed product/service brief was prepared. £10–15,000. The many services covered by the research company fell in the fee range £10–17,000.

For a small firm with limited financial resources, there are lower cost methods, and for those firms with ambitions to export, a considerable amount of help available through government agencies at low cost, or free.

Other Survey Methods

Omnibus surveys ask questions on behalf of many different client companies and thus cut costs since the individual client pays only for his or her particular questions. Several research firms conduct surveys on a regular basis and client companies list their questions and receive the answers, usually in the form of a computer print-out. The surveys are carried out by personal interview or telephone. General omnibus surveys and specialist surveys are available and the former interview is a representative sample of 1000–2000 people on a regular weekly or monthly basis. Because some clients may require less than the whole sample, or require a sample, for example, composed of females only (such as housewives) this can be made available at a lower cost.

Specialist surveys are sold to companies who are interested in a specific market sector; farmers, motorists etc. Omnibus surveys allow a firm to test the reaction to a modified product or a new method of packaging. The use of a regular omnibus survey will allow a firm to gauge if it is gaining market share and if so from whom, or alternatively, who else is reducing its market share.

Most omnibus survey providers charge an initial entry fee followed by a charge per question asked. Help is offered by the survey firms in designing the form of question, the initial fee is payable usually on a once-only basis. For general omnibus surveys using personal interviews the entry fee is of the order of £100. Telephone surveys as well as some specialist surveys do not charge an entry fee.

The prices charged for questions depends upon:

- The size of sample required
- The number of questions to be asked
- The number of people answering
- The type of question to be asked

General omnibus surveys charge £150–250 per question for 'pre-coded' questions and for specialist surveys £90–350. A list of some of the firms who carry out general omnibus surveys, is given below:

Survey	Firm	Frequency	Entry Fee	Cost/precoded question (sample of 1000)
Access	British Market Research Bureau	Weekly	£100	£165
Gallup omnibus	Social Surveys	Weekly	£195	£170
GB omnibus	Market & Opinion Research	Fortnightly	£140	£190
Household survey	Survey force	Monthly	sometimes	£140
Random omnibus	NOP Market Research	Weekly	£130	£230
Telephone omnibus (Telephone survey)	NOP Market Research	Weekly	None	£225

Specialist surveys carried out less frequently than general surveys are offered by firms such as Martin-Hamblin

Research's Mediline for medical and pharmaceutical matters, samples GP's. The same firm's Telepharm uses a telephone panel of 250 retail pharmacists; prices are £90 to question 200 GP's plus £450 entry fee. Taylor Nelson's Pharmacy Pointer charges £200 per question and a £200 entry fee. Travel and Tourism Research offer a Travel Agent's Omnibus Survey: 20 agents and minimum fee £500. Produce Studies Omnifarm is a panel of 1000 farmers, minimum fee £500. Research surveys of Great Britain offers a Motering Omnibus; 1000 motorists, entry fee £150 and £250 per question. Many survey providers exist and a list of addresses is given in the reference section.

Other Sources

Firms seeking the answers to questions addressed to other business can use:

- Key Directors Omnibus from Audience Selection, a quarterly survey of 600 decision-makers from the top British businesses.
- Telebus from Market Research Enterprises (a quarterly telephone survey of 1200 business people)
- Business Line from Business Decisions who question 2000 small businesses.

Omnibus surveys are less costly than commissioning a market research firm with a specific brief. If the firm requires answers to a large number of questions however, an omnibus survey can be costly. Respondents to a specially commissioned questionnaire are in fact concentrating solely on the questions specifically required by the firm and in this sense can be more effective. The omnibus survey providers will not give the degree of assistance normally offered by a firm commissioned specially in the sense of helping with the basics of formulating the (buying firms) correct questions and discussing in detail the implications of the findings.

Omnibus surveys are of no value in extracting information from certain very specialised groups where no such survey exists but for a relatively low cost (under £1000) an omnibus survey will obtain answers to a limited number of questions asked by professional market research practitioners.

Assistance with Market Research for Export Markets

As an introduction to exporting, the Small Firm's Service offer a free and very useful booklet 'How to start Exporting' which can be obtained free by telephoning Freefone 2444. A good deal of literature is also available from the main High Street Banks, which deal with export finance, foreign exchange, letters of credit and associated topics. Local export clubs can also provide valuable information and practical help.

The British Overseas Trade Board (BOTB) is a good source of information and provides free booklets on many overseas markets giving detailed information which is regularly updated. There is currently available, free of charge, from the BOTB a new edition of its Export Wall Map which shows all British diplomatic posts offering commercial services. This useful map can be obtained from the nearest BOTB regional office.

Foreign Embassies and Consulates are another useful source of market information and can, if properly asked, save a firm's time and money in researching the market abroad for its products or services.

The Statistics and Market Intelligence Library at the Department of Trade and Industry is a source of information about the needs of countries overseas and their development plans and this can be invaluable to the exporter. Also at this London based library, is the BOTB's Product Data Store which provides data on very many products around the world. The data is stored under 3000 different product headings according to the Standard Industrial Classification.

The BOTB can very much reduce the effort on the part of the firm's ambitions to export and who wish to find the potential for their product in specific countries. The Market Prospects Service and Export Representative Service have been profitably used by firms starting to export and needing information on the prospects for their product or service, competing products, identifying potential customers as well as advice on price, quality and distribution methods. The reports cost less than £200 and if the firm is encouraged to visit the country this fee is refunded as a contribution to travel costs. Full details of this service can be obtained from the nearest BOTB office.

The Export Representative Service will give assistance in selecting agents and distributors in a particular country. This service is very cheap and again the fee is refunded should the firm visit the country to visit the recommended agent(s).

Market Research at low cost is available through the BOTB's Export Marketing Research Scheme. The scheme contributes to the cost of market research commissioned from consultants, and a contribution to travel costs for employees of the firm carrying out research outside the EEC as well as substantial financial help towards research commissioned by trade associations. Details of help available and impartial advice on researching overseas markets can be obtained from the Export Marketing Research Section at 1 Victoria Street, London SW1H OET.

Having chosen a potential overseas representative to handle the firm's product or service, the BOTB can supply at very low cost, an assessment of the agent or distributor through its Overseas Status Report Service. This report, obtainable from the local BOTB office, gives detail of the interests and capabilities of the overseas company, its commercial standing, territorial coverage and facilities.

Further help is available from The British Standards Institution from its department which supplies Help to Exporters, giving information on foreign standards and requirements; a translation service is also available. Some help is given free of charge but the BSI will charge for detailed research. Information and help from this service can be obtained from BSI, Longford Wood, Milton Keynes MK14 6LE.

A useful article by Professor T. Faulkner titled 'Researching Your Market on a Small Budget' is included in The National Westminster Bank's Small Business Digest, issue No. 26, July 1987. This short paper draws attention to the two kinds of research, Desk Research and Field Research and lists sources of information already in existence for the smaller business through:

- Libraries
- Trade Associations, Chamber of Commerce
- CBI Industrial Training Boards etc.
- Central Government Departments
- Local Government Departments
- Banks
- Special agencies which exist to help small firms
- Newspapers such as The Financial Times
- Specialist trade and other magazines
- Suppliers/Customers

This list whilst not exhaustive does offer an indication of the wide range of free or low cost sources of available information. Brief but pertinent comments on Field Research are also included in this article which concludes with the statement that, "Marketing Research takes time, even money, but so does the failure which can result from poorly informed marketing decisions!"

SUMMARY

With the increasing acceptance of the marketing concept which places customer needs at the centre of the organisation's activities, research to determine these needs in detail has expanded enormously over recent years. In communication terms it is the vital feedback of information into the organisation which enables it to adapt rapidly and accurately to changes in its market environment and to substantially reduce the degree of risk associated with the launch of new products.

- It is scientific and logical
- It has clear objectives
- A variety of data sources are used, both primary and secondary sources are important

- Great care should be taken in the design of questionnaires
- Outside agencies may provide greater expertise and be less biased towards a desired outcome
- It provides the feedback to ensure effective communication

REFERENCES AND FURTHER READING

1. Research Associates, Stone, Staffordshire.
2. The Industrial Market Research Society, Bird Street, Lichfield, Staffs.
3. Tupper & Mills 1975. Sources of UK Marketing Information, Ernest Benn.
4. Government Statistics. A Brief Guide to Sources. HMSO.
5. The Economist Intelligence Unit, 27 St. James Place, London SW1.
6. Mintel Publications, 20 Buckingham Street, London WC2N 6BR.
7. The IPC Consumer & Industrial Marketing Manual. IPC Publications. The Market Research Society, 37 Hertford Street, London.
8. Statistics & Marketing Intelligence Library, 50 Ludgate Hill, London EC8 7HU.
9. Trade & Industry (Weekly) HMSO London.

REFERENCE ADDRESSES

Audience Selection, 10–14 Macklin Street, London WC2B 5NF.
British Market Research Bureau Ltd., 53 The Mall, Ealing, London W5 3TE.
Business Decisions, 25 Wellington Street, London WC2E 7DW.
Carrick James Market Research, 11 Great Marlborough Street, London W1.

Harris Research Centre, Holbrooke House, Holbrooke Place, 34–38 Hill Rise, Richmond, Surrey TW10 6UA.

Market & Opinion Research International, 32 Old Queen Street, London SW1H 9HP.

Marplan Ltd., Bridgewater House, 5–13 Great Suffolk Street, London SE1 0NS.

Martin-Hamblin Research, Mulberry House, 36 Smith Square, London SW1P 3HL.

NOP Market Research Ltd., Tower House, Southampton Street, London WC2E.

Research Surveys of Great Britain Ltd. Research Centre, West Gate, London W5 1EL.

Sample Surveys Ltd., 82 Bishops Bridge Road, London W2 6BB.

Social Surveys (Gallup Poll) Ltd., 202 Finchley Road, London NW3.

Taylor Nelson Medical, 44–46 Upper High Street, Epsom, Surrey KT17 4QS.

Travel & Tourism Research, Lector Court, 151–153 Farringdon Road, London EC1R 3AD.

CHAPTER 15

SOURCES OF FURTHER INFORMATION AND ASSISTANCE

Introduction

This chapter summarises the help currently available to firms wishing to improve their marketing effectiveness and other aspects of marketing. A list of definitions and notes on marketing terms is given together with a further reading list of marketing texts and articles under appropriate headings.

Support for Marketing (SFM)

SFM is a DTI scheme aimed at helping small/medium sized firms to get expert advice on how they can raise their marketing effectiveness and performance to the level achieved by the most successful UK and international businesses.

This important initiative by the Department of Trade and Industry's Business and Technical Advisory Services is managed by the Chartered Institute of Marketing on behalf of the DTI.

Support Offered

Firms can obtain up to 15 days of marketing assistance from a specialist marketing consultant. There is no charge for the first two days during which time a survey is carried out and details of the proposed assignment prepared. For the remainder the firm is charged at one third of the cost, the balance being met by the DTI. The minimum time for a project is eight days of assistance. The service is confidential and no work is disclosed without the firm's approval.

Support is available to independent firms or groups anywhere in Great Britain with 1—500 employees. Each firm is entitled to one assisted project only.

Qualifying Criteria

To qualify for assistance the firm needs to demonstrate that any project forms part of a sound business plan and the benefits will lead to an increase in international competitiveness in a reasonable timescale.

The SFM initiative itself is aimed at companies which require assistance in developing their marketing strategies and overall marketing plan, as opposed to one of the elements of marketing.

There are no application forms and request for further information can be made either to the Chartered Institute of Marketing or one of the four other contact points listed below:

HEAD OFFICE   The Chartered Institute of Marketing Moor Hall
Cookham
Maidenhead
Berks SL6 9QH
Tel. (062 85) 24922
Telex: 849462
Fax. (062 85) 31382

SCOTLAND   University of Strathclyde
Stenhouse Building
173 Cathedral Street
Glasgow G4 0RG
Tel. 041–552 4400

THE NORTH	Salford University Business Expansion Services Limited
	Salbee House
	Salford
	M6 6GS
	Tel. 061–736 2843
MIDLANDS &	University of Warwick
SOUTH WEST	School of Industrial and Business Studies
	Coventry
	CV4 7AL
	Tel. 0203 523523
SOUTH &	Marketing and Logistics Group
SOUTH EAST	Cranfield School of Marketing
	Cranfield
	Bedford
	MK43 0AL
	Tel. 0234 751122

Information and advice on the Government assistance schemes can be obtained from the DTI's regional office.

Grants from Europe for Small Firms

Other grants and help are available through the European Regional Development Fund and the Department of Trade and Industry. They are available to:

- people setting up in business
- independent small firms employing up to 200 people or part of a group employing that number
- consultants, or any kind of organisation, providing a service to small firms.

Grants include:

- 55% grants towards the cost of a business check up to establish key areas for improvement and possibly identify the need for specific follow-up consultancy work

- 70% grants towards the cost of reviewing a firm's marketing activities and drawing up of a marketing strategy for the future.
- 55% grants towards the cost of:
  a) Translations of marketing information and sales literature from or into foreign languages
  b) Advise on improving existing budget and control systems
  c) Licensing-in new product
  d) Investigate the merits of acquiring a micro- computer
- 70% grant towards the cost of feasibility projects leading to the development of new products and processes.

Details about these grants and the financial limits imposed can be obtained by contacting the Regional Office of the Department of Trade and Industry nearest to the firm.

Regional Development Grants

The extent of assistance now varies according to the designation of the geographical area. Prior to November 1984, the three categories of Development Area were:—

- Special Development Areas (SDAs)
- Development Areas (DAs)
- Intermediate Areas (IAs)

SDAs were the areas with the most serious problems of structural decline such as Merseyside, Clydeside and Newcastle, and they received the greatest assistance. The scale of assistance was less in the DAs and IAs. Nothern Ireland was categorised as an SDA receiving additional assistance because of unique problems in that region. In November 1984 the category of special development area was dispensed with leaving only:

- Development Areas
- Intermediate Areas

MAP 1

Map 1 above shows the distribution of the development areas.

Prior to March 1988 the main instrument of Regional Policy was the Regional Development Grant (RDG). The RDG was a capital grant of 15% payable to firms in the Development Areas for investment in plant, buildings and machinery. The grants were subject to a cost per job limit of £10,000. Alternatively a job grant was made available of £3,000 for each new job created in labout intensive projects.

Capital grants were subject to the criticism that they encouraged capital intensive production when the underlying purpose was the creation of jobs. Also, the grants failed to discriminate between good and bad investment and the grant would be paid to firms who would have made the investment even if the grant did not exist.

To overcome some of these criticisms the government introduced in March 1988 The Regional Initiative with a new system of Regional Enterprise Grants. The new system of grants are given at the discretion of the Department of Trade and Industry (DTI) upon the presentation of a business plan by the applicant and are therefore no longer automatically available. The grants will be provided only if the business plan meets the criteria of the DTI, and the project is taking place in a Development Area or South Yorkshire.

The criteria applied include: market opportunities for the business over the next 2—3 years, the effect of the project on sales, profits and employment levels, and how the project and the business will be financed.

a.— grants for investment projects in most manufacturing and some service sectors. The DTI will pay 15% of expenditure on fixed assets in the project, up to a maximum grant of £15,000. Eligible costs include plant and machinery (new or second hand), buildings, purchase of land and site preparation and vehicles used solely on site and;

b.— grants for innovation projects which lead to the development and introduction of new or improved products and processes. The DTI will pay 50% of eligible costs, up to a maximum grant of £25,000. Work can range from feasability studies through the development of technical specifications, to the design and manufacture of prototypes. There is no limit on the size of projects which can be considered.

The measures introduced in March 1988 represent a significant movement towards a more market oriented approach to regional policy. However, readers are advised to consult the DTI about these measures as they are subject to rapid change.

Tax Allowances

Tax allowances for capital expenditure on building, plant and machinery are available and details of current rates of first year and initial allowances will be given by the local Inspector of Taxes.

Small firms having difficulty in obtaining finance for starting up or expanding due to insufficient security can be helped by the Loan Guarantee Scheme from the government. Details can be obtained by contacting any High Street Bank or Industrial and Commercial Finance Corporation Limited (ICFC).

For firms located in a rural area or country town where the population is under 10,000 aid can be received through the Council for Small Industries in Rural Areas (COSIRA) towards loans for buildings, equipment, raw materials and working capital. Firms should contact their nearest COSIRA office.

Assistance for Research and Development in New Technology and support for innovation is available in many areas. Again, contact with the DTI Regional Office will establish what aid is available in the area of operation of the firm or research organisation. The applying company must be viable and have the technical and financial capability to carry the development through. The project must be innovative, stand a good chance of success, and, improve the company's performance. No assistance is given if the project is able to proceed without Government support.

Schemes for consultancy help and aid towards feasability studies are available in many areas and the DTI Regional Office will supply details.

Assistance for Adult Training, Tourism Projects and help towards the cost of employing a specialist consultant to carry out a survey aimed at Energy Conservation is available in many areas, again, details are available form the DTI or County Central Offices.

A guide to Local Authority Assistance is published by the National Westminster Bank Plc in the form of several directories and these are obtainable from:

National Westminster Bank Plc
Commercial Information Section

6th Floor
National House
14 Moorgate
LONDON
EC24 6BS

Under various acts, Local Authorities have certain general powers by which they are able to provide assistance in industry where this lies in the interest of their own locality. These include help with mortgage loans for the acquisition of, or the carrying out of works on land and, with the consent of the Secretary of State, the disposal of land below market value. Other assistance may include improvement grants, industrial site preparation and provision of advance factories.

The ways in which Local Authorities operate vary widely. Each council determines the kind of assistance it will offer and the amount it will allocate for such measures, according to the needs of its own area. The National Westminster Bank publications provide a very useful guide to business in all areas who should keep in close touch with their local authority for up to date information and changes that may affect them.

Many publications from local authorities, the DTI and other government agencies dealing with both financial and other forms of assistance are available and the amount of information available is enormous. Many large accountancy firms, as well as high street banks, can provide summaries of information available. Some specialist firms however can not only provide this information and advise client companies accordingly but are willing and able, for a fee, to make the detailed application on behalf of client companies and, because of their daily contact with government and local authority officials, deal with the considerable detail and information required on the way to securing the appropriate grant(s). Individuals or firms seeking detailed help in these areas who lack the time, or experience, to deal with the complexities of deciding what help is available to them or are unable to cope with the detailed application requirements are advised to shop around for organisations who have in-depth experience in this area.

Publications referring to financial aid to industry and

commerce from county councils, banks, accounting firms and the STI changed in 1988 and the reader should take account of this when seeking help.

REFERENCES

1. Financial Aid to Commerce and Industry, Employment Promotion Group, Cheshire County Council, Commerce House, Hunter Street, Chester, CH1 1SN (February 1988).
2. New Sources of Grants, WEKA Publishing Limited, The Forum, 74—80 Camden Street, London, NW1 0EG.
3. Finance T, NW Business Monthly, September 1986.
4. Industry North West, March 1989.
5. The Chartered Institute of Management Accountants, September — December 1987.
6. A Directory of Grant Making Trusts, published by Charities and Foundations, 48 Penbury Road, Tonbridge, Kent, TN9 2JD.
7. Cheshire County Council Economic Development Service, Shipgate House, Shipgate Street, Chester, CH1 1RT.

CHAPTER 16

GLOSSARY OF MARKETING TERMS

ADVERTISING ASSOCIATION: Established in 1926 to promote public confidence in advertising maintain standards and generally look after the interest of the industry.

BRAND AWARENESS: Much advertising has, as its main object the creation and reinforcement of brand awareness — ie the public's awareness of a given product brand. This is all the more important if the product has little apart from its packing and image to distinguish it from other equally good rivals.

BRIEF: Instructions telling the agency about the product, the market and the purpose of the proposed advertising. Generally provided by the account executive on the basis of discussions woth the client. The clearer and more comprehensive the brief, the better the advertising is likely to be.

BUSINESS LIST: Any list of individuals or companies based upon a business-associated interest, inquiry, membership, subscription or purchase.

CHESHIRE LABEL: Specially prepared paper used to reproduce names and addresses to be mechanically affixed, one at a time, to a mailing list.

COMPETITION-ORIENTATED PRICING: is used by firms who set prices on the basis of what their competitors are charging.

COMPILED LIST: Names and addresses derived from directories, newspapers, public records, retail sales slips, tradeshow registrations etc, to identify groups of people with something in common.

CONSUMER LIST: A list of names and home address of people who have bought merchandise, subscriptions, services, etc via mail, radio or television.

CONVERSION: Many mailings and direct response ads want their audience in the first instance to send for a brochure, further information, a salesman's visit etc. The cost-effectiveness depends not on the mere response rate but on the number of respondents when they go on to actually buy, ie the number of conversions from expression of interest to actual purchase.

CO-OP MAILING: A mailing in which two or more offers are included in the same envelope (or other carrier) and share costs according to a predetermined formula.

COST-PLUS PRICING: is used to price products or jobs that are non-routine and difficult to 'cost' in advance, eg construction and development work.

COST-RELATED PRICING: systems are used by firms to set prices mainly on the basis of cost. All costs are included together with an allocation of overheads based on expected production levels.

DATABASE: A number of lists with a common interest merged into one master list thus eliminating duplication.

DEMOGRAPHICS: Socio-economic characters pertaining to a geographic unit (country, city, sectional centre, group of households etc).

DIRECT RESPONSE ADVERTISING AGENCY OR DIRECT MARKETING AGENCY:

A direct marketing agency acts as a full service advertising agency but specialises in the direct marketing business. A direct marketing agency does not specialise in direct mail but employs whatever media are required — press, broadcasts media, mail inserts, telephone — to execute a direct marketing campaign.

GEOGRAPHICS: Any method of subdividing a list, based on geographic locations.

HOUSE LIST: Any list of names owned by a company as a result of inquiry, or acquisition.

LIST BROKER: One who provides industries with ready

prepared lists that are rented from him or her by the selling organisation and are provided by other industries in the same field.

LIST EXCHANGE: A barter arrangement between two companies for the use of a mailing list(s).

LIST MAINTENANCE: Any manual, mechanical or electronic system for keeping names and address records (with or without other data) so that they are up to date at any point in time.

LIST OWNER: One who, by promotional activity or compilation, has developed a list of names having something in common — or one who has purchased (as opposed to rented, reproduced, or used on a one-time basis) such a list from the developer.

LIST SELECTION: Characteristics used to define smaller groups within a list (essentially lists, within a list). Although very small, select groups may be very desirable and may substantially improve response, increased costs often render them impractical.

LIST SOURCE: The media (general or specific) used to generate names on a mailing list.

LIST TEST: A part of a list selected to try to determine the effectiveness of the entire list (A List Sample).

MERGE: Combining of two or more lists (or two or more segments of the same list) — usually in a predetermined sequence.

MERGE/PURGE: Combining two or more list or units and eliminating duplication at the same time.

MAIL PREFERENCE SERVICES (MPS): A service that enables consumers to have their names and addresses removed from or added to mailing lists.

MAILING HOUSES: There are a number of descriptions for companies specialising in providing direct mail production and sometimes fulfilment services. Such companies are broadly labelled 'Producer Houses' but the term 'Lettershop' an 'American' expression, is also common. In fact, 'Lettershop' specifically refers to the inserting of mailing pieces which can include labelling.

When using a Mailing House, one should check:

1. The capability of the company to handle the work being placed with it;
2. The back up production controls, both physical and written;
3. Efficient reporting both during work processing and on completion, plus dedication to meeting deadlines. Satisfactory communication;
4. Quality of personnel one is dealing with — one must have confidence in them and;
5. Cleanliness of works and equipment.

A good mailing house must provide all these services in depth or, if it specialises in one service, have adequate knowledge and facilities available to provide if efficiently. The Direct Mail Service Industry still consists of a relatively small number of companies and they can easily be checked out through the various Associations.

There is even a science to putting things into envelopes. Direct mail houses can tell you the most economical ways to use different types of labels, envelopes or even folding material that goes into envelopes. Talk to a few. Get quotes and find the most efficient.

MARGINAL COST PRICING: Manufacturing costs may be divided into fixed and variable, the latter vary according to output and the former remain unchanged regardless of the level of activity. When output produces sufficient revenue to cover fixed and variable costs, it has reached 'break-even' point. When a firm can find a customer, isolated market, or segment without jeopardising price levels in existing markets, it can quote prices based on marginal costs. Additional sales increase total profit although percentage profit per unit will be lower. Marginal pricing provides a reason for accepting the lowest possible price but is a dangerous practice when uncontrolled

MARKETING: Several definitions are common, but only two are reproduced here. Marketing is a management process responsible for anticipating and satisfying client and customer needs — at a profit. Marketing is a total business philosophy aimed at improving profit performance, through identifying customer needs, designing the best service or product to satisfy these needs, delivering the offering on time and providing a sound after-sales service.

MARKETING AUDIT: is a systematic, critical and objective anlysis of a firm's marketing capability and the environment in which it operates. The main job of the audit is to examine internal strengths and weakness and analyse the external situation.

MARKETING MIX: refers to the main variables available to the firm in order to match the benefits sought by buyers with those offered by the seller. The firm's marketing mix (the "4P's") is represented by PRODUCT, PRICE, PROMOTION, AND PLACE (distribution service).

MARKETING OBJECTIVES: are statements of targets to be pursued and achieved during the period covered by the marketing plan. Objectives relating to profit, market share, market development and penetration are primary objectives, more commonly called strategic or business objectives since they relate to the objectives of the firm as a whole. Objectives set for specific marketing activities can be described as programme objectives.

MARKETING PLAN: A marketing plan for any company relates solely to that company and sets down:

- Where the firm is now;
- Where the firm wishes to go and;
- How is should organise its resources to do it.

The elements of the plan are a marketing audit or SWOT analysis, a statement of some key assumptions, marketing objectives, strategies and programmes for each level of the business.

MARKET RESEARCH: the process of systematic investigation into markets to:
a) Establish present and potential demand for consumer and industrial products and;
b) To provide a basis for management decisions.

MARKET SEGMENTATION: is concerned with distinguishing relevant customer groups and their needs and interests. This is not concerned with distinguishing product or service possibilities.

MARKET SHARE: The percentage of the market represented by a firm's sales in relation to total sales.

MARKET SKIMMING PRICING: takes advantage of the fact that some buyers are ready to pay a higher price than others since the product or service has a high value to them. This situation can be advantageous if there are enough buyers whose demand is relatively inelastic, small volume production is not expensive and there is little danger of entry by rival firms.

NEGOTIATION: The process by which two parties reach a mutually acceptable agreement through the means of trade and concession.

PENETRATION PRICING: is aimed at stimulating market growth to capture a larger share of the market and is likely to be used if the market is highly price sensitive.

POLICIES: are summary statements of objectives and strategies.

PRODUCT LIFE CYCLE: describes the birth, growth, maturity and decline of a product over time. During the life of a product, sales income increases and then declines. Profitability will depend on the marketer's approach in manipulating the market mix during its life. Total life expectancy of products varies enormously and efforts, during launch and thereafter, to extend the life cycle and profitability require considerable creativity on the part of the producer.

PRODUCT/SERVICE POSITIONING: Good marketing requires the selling company to give its products a real or psychological difference from that of competing products since buyers make their choice from a competitive field. A differentiated product is one that is seen by buyers as particularly suited to their needs compared with competing products. The selling company needs to:

- show that its product satisfies the need of those buyers within particular segments and;
- find the best position in the 'product space' with respect to competitors and lead buyers to believe that this is the product that most accurately meets his needs.

PROGRAMMES: details of the final steps in marketing planning, listing the tasks to to be undertaken by all participating departments in line with the strategies and objectives and previously set down. Programmes define the individuals or departments responsible for achieving objectives listed in a given time period.

PROTECTION: The amount of time before and after the assigned mailing date, during which the list owner will not allow the same names to be mailed to anyone other than the mailer cleared for that specific date.

PSYCHOLOGICAL PRICING: When the seller (eg retailer) reduces the price down to a level just below a supposed 'barrier' price for example £9.95 is possibly more attractive than £10.

RESPONSE: The replies that come in as a result of a mailing, TV promotion or sales drive.

ROLL OUT: The number of names ordered after a test mailing.

S.I.C. (Standard Industrial Classifications). Business catergories defined by the Central Statistical Office (C.S.O.).

SAMPLE PACKAGE (MAILING PIECE): An example of the package to be mailed by the list user to a particular list. Such a mailing piece is submitted to the list owner for approval prior to commitment for one-item use of that list.

SATISFICING: occurs when a company is satisfied with a price because is is considered conventional for a given level of risk despite the possibility of an increased return.

SELF ADHESIVE LABEL: A label that can be removed from a sheet and affixed to an envelope or another address carrrier.

SOURCE/KEY CODE: A group of letters and/or numbers, colours, other marking used to measure the specific effectiveness of the media, lists, advertisements, offers ect.

SPLIT TEST: Two or more samples from the same list — each considered to be representative of the entire list — used for package tests or to test the homogeneity of the list.

STANDARD COSTING: is the ascertaining and utilising of standard costs (predetermined costs) and the measurement and analysis of variances (variance analysis is the resolution into component parts, and the explanation of variances).

TARGET: Objectives set for an individual or group eg the group's target is to increases sales by x% to hardware retailers.

TARGET PRICING: is a cost-orientated approach where the producer decides the price that will give a rate of return on total costs at a budgeted level in line with the financial objectives set by the company's board.

TARGET AUDIENCE: The audience at which an advertiser aims their advertising. One of direct mail's great strengths is its selectivity which enables the advertisers to reach their target audience with great accuracy.

UNIQUE NAMES: The names that appear on one list only after a merge/page process has been completed. A unique name differs from a duplicate name in this respect, although each is used once only in a particular mailing.

INDEX